民间故事

Chinese Folktales

Howard Giskin

Appalachian State University

NTC Publishing Group
Lincolnwood, Illinois USA

P9-DLZ-647

This book is dedicated to my wife, Vicki; my parents, Bernice and
Henry Giskin; my sisters, Rosalie and Lynelle, and my brother, Steve.

Executive Editor: John T. Nolan
Project Manager: Nancy Liskar
Cover design: Cunningham & Welch Design Group
Interior design: Ophelia M. Chambliss
Production Manager: Rosemary Dolinski

Library of Congress Cataloging-in-Publication Data

Giskin, Howard, 1956–
    Chinese folktales / Howard Giskin.
        p.   cm.
    ISBN 0-8442-5927-6
    1. Tales—China.   2. Tales—China—Classification.   I. Title.
GR335.G54 1996
398.2'0951—dc20   96-7983
                                                              CIP

Published by NTC Publishing Group.
©1997 NTC Publishing Group, 4255 West Touhy Avenue,
Lincolnwood (Chicago), Illinois 60646-1975 U.S.A.
All Rights Reserved. No part of this book may be reproduced, stored
in a retrieval system, or transmitted in any form or by any means,
electronic, mechanical, photocopying, recording or otherwise, without
the prior permission of NTC Publishing Group.
Manufactured in the United States of America.

6 7 8 9 VP 9 8 7 6 5 4 3 2 1

Contents

Fairy Tales and Fables   181

Preface

During the fall and spring of 1993–94, my wife Vicki and I spent an academic year teaching at Northeast University in the People's Republic of China. We were delighted to have the chance to share many wonderful experiences with our Chinese hosts, and most of all to work with a wide range of Chinese students, who surprised us in many ways. The students' grasp of written English was surprisingly strong, which facilitated our gathering of folktales.

Northeast University is a large, technology-oriented institution in the city of Shenyang, Liaoning Province, some four hundred miles north of Beijing. Historically known as Manchuria, the region is now referred to by the Chinese simply as the Northeast, comprising the provinces of Liaoning, Jilin, and Heilongjiang. Shenyang, which used to go by the Manchu name of Mukden, is the seat of heavy industry in Northeast China.

This book grew out of our conviction that there are many Chinese tales that have yet to be made available to the English-speaking world. Because of our students' varied places of origin, we were able to gather stories from every region of the country except the Tibetan High Plateau, which constitutes an entirely different ethno-linguistic zone. Many students came from cities, towns, or villages that are scarcely known outside of China, and their stories often concern geographic features or local monuments that would hardly be known outside a small region, village, or town.

The number of folktales in China is enormous, and I am not aware that anyone has ever attempted to catalog or even to count them. The impossibility of such a task becomes clear when one realizes that nearly every unusual landmark or geographical feature has at least one story associated with it, sometimes a number of variations on the same story. The Chinese are very fond of such tales, telling them to their children, their grandchildren, and even their friends.

All of the stories in this collection were recounted orally in Chinese and were written down in English by our students. Though I rephrased these tales into idiomatic English, our students collected and translated these stories. We are grateful for their cooperation and no doubt painstaking work at writing in a foreign language. We are also grateful to the grandmothers and grandfathers, mothers and fathers, and others who took the trouble to tell these stories, thus preserving them for another generation of Chinese people and now, for readers of English.

Liaoning Province is most heavily represented in these stories, though there are a number of tales from the provinces of Hubei, Henan, Hebei, Shandong, and Zhejiang. Beijing and Shanghai, which are separate administrative regions, and the provinces of Guizhou, Guangxi, Qinghai, Gansu, Shanxi, Hainan, and Shaanxi are each represented by one story, while other provinces provided a varying number of tales. In an effort to keep the students' voices alive, we asked them to begin their narration with a short section on their hometown and province, as well as how they heard their tale. We hope that this information will be interesting and useful, and that it will give readers a better sense of the sociocultural background from which these stories came.

Collecting these stories has been an education in the enduring wealth of the Chinese culture, a culture that is likely to continue to influence global civilization for generations to come.

Acknowledgments

I would like to thank Professor Xie Xukai and his wife, Luo Yongfei, for their friendship and kindness while my wife and I were in China. I would also like to express my appreciation to Appalachian State University's Marvin Williamsen, director of international studies, and Thomas Adams, assistant director of international studies, for their support before and during our stay in China. Nancy Liskar, my editor at NTC, offered advice and suggestions that made this a better book. I am especially grateful to the Chinese students who so willingly shared the folktales that comprise this volume.

Introduction

Folktales perform a useful function in China, acting as a cultural web in what has been—and still is in part—a semiliterate country. Partial literacy is a difficulty for a nation working to enter the modern world. However, the continued reliance, at least in the countryside, on oral communication means that many of the old stories continue to be told. In this respect China is somewhat unusual in modern times, for it is an established fact that the spread of literacy and the abandoning of traditional ways of life often signal the decline, if not the end, of folk traditions.

Attempts to modernize the Chinese culture have been somewhat successful at bringing the benefits of economic development to rural China. In many areas, however, farmers continue to live much as they have for generations, and many of the stories in this collection come from rural areas. Though the survival of such folktales seems assured for now, we cannot help wondering about the fate of this oral tradition as China moves inexorably into the twenty-first century.

The Chinese love to create stories about their world. Bridges, mountains, rivers, weather, and even odd-looking stones and other natural formations have their own tales, stories that somehow lend these objects a life of their own. There is something comforting in the richness that this storytelling creates; seldom do the people who know and live these stories feel the emptiness that seems to characterize modern life.

The stories in this volume are presented thematically, because that seemed the best way to allow readers to appreciate the scope and range of Chinese storytelling. Beginning with a section on dragon lore also seemed appropriate, considering the pervasiveness of the dragon in Chinese culture. Following the dragon tales are stories about love and magic, as well as sections on supernatural beings, history and legend, fairy tales and, finally, human nature.

Dragon Tales

Stories about dragons have played a part in Chinese culture for thousands of years. As early as the Shang Dynasty (c. 1523–1122 B.C.), the dragon appeared as a symbol of supernatural power. The legend of the dragon may have originated when early peoples found the fossilized remains of extinct animals that had roamed China in ancient times. However these stories began, the dragon has fascinated the Chinese for centuries.

Over time dragons came to represent divine power, which, as the Chinese well knew, could help or hurt humans. Some of the dragons in the stories in this section are good and work to make people's lives better, while others wreak havoc on towns and villages for the sheer pleasure of seeing villagers suffer. It is difficult to know precisely what dragons meant to all of the Chinese throughout the ages. From a folk perspective, however, they provided an explanation for certain natural phenomena that caused difficulties for a people closely tied to the land.

Love

Chinese folktales about love often, but not always, end sadly. One can speculate about why this is. The constraints of traditional Chinese society made romantic love a distant dream for most. Because marriages were arranged, with little or no consent by the parties to be wed, it is not surprising that relationships based exclusively on love were rare. Yet the persistence of the theme of true love suggests that, despite the harsh constraints, romantic attachments did form, sometimes with such power and passion that the couple threw off considerations of propriety and family. The results, unfortunately, were often tragic.

Magic

The stories in this section show magic positively, as a force for exposing greed or highlighting moral goodness. The aim of magic as it is presented here is not to control nature, but to cooperate with unusual events that are nevertheless part of the naturally occurring scheme of things. In each of the stories, magic works to the advantage of those who use it wisely. Clearly, those who abuse the miracles nature has to offer are likely to suffer unpleasant results. The stories here show with a light touch what other tales more ominously detail—that using the forces of nature for evil or greedy gain brings only ruin.

Ghosts, Monsters, and Evil Spirits

These stories recount a wide variety of destructive forces—both natural and psychological—in the lives of Chinese people. Myth and folklore tend to externalize and personify, presenting us with visual images that embody certain aspects in a people's environment. While it is not necessary to classify each monster or demon, physically destructive creatures typically represent nature and its ability to cause chaos: wind, rain, storms, volcanoes, earthquakes, and floods. Early peoples knew these dangers well, and even today we are subject to the awesome, unpredictable forces of the world around us.

Demons, ghosts, and evil spirits appear to represent a combination of internal and external forces. Anyone who has spent a night camped in a tent by the side of a lonely road, slept in a house said to be haunted, or felt the eerie quiet of the inky black forest beyond a campfire knows that—try as we might to stay calm, powerful, irrational forces bubble up into our consciousness. It is easy to think that ancient peoples, or for that matter the villagers who invented these stories, had the same reactions. Perhaps creating these stories was a way for people to make sense of the mysterious forces that governed their lives and—by naming and describing them—to gain a measure of control.

History and Legend

A number of the stories in this section deal with events that have some historical basis in fact but have been molded to fit the requirements of folktales. First and foremost is the narrator's desire to tell a good story that, while factually true in some aspects, keeps the reader's or listener's attention and creates a sense of satisfaction at its conclusion. These folktales can teach us not only about historical events, but perhaps more importantly, about the Chinese perception of these events.

The stories presented in this section do not merely record events said to have happened (this would be meaningless, I believe, to the Chinese), but are moral narratives through which people strive to make sense of what resides in their memories. For the Chinese, history is a treasurehouse of good and evil, of heroes and villains, of the wise and foolish, of emperors and peasants; often the distant past is as relevant as yesterday. Qin Shihuangdi, the brilliant but brutal first emperor of a unified China, stands alongside such modern figures as Mao Zedong and Zhou Enlai as a measure of the Chinese character, while Confucius, great poets, political leaders, generals, and artisans are frequently seen as models for today.

While not all of the stories in this section refer to identifiable events from the past, they do all show a cultural tradition in which memory plays a key role. Even in stories that are clearly more legend than history, we may wonder at the roots of the folktale; it is just possible that in some place, in some form, in some ancient kingdom, the events of the story did take place.

Fairy Tales and Fables

The stories in this section represent a selection of what China has to offer in the genre of the fantastic. Here you will find tales that stretch the limits of imagination, at the same time tapping into the common human experience. Some of these stories teach us about the limits of life, about the inevitable sorrows we must all face, while others draw from the vast source of hope that lies like a subterranean reservoir just under the surface of Chinese life.

Not all of the stories in this section end happily, and several leave us wondering at the injustices of life. These tales remind us that the satisfaction of desires can be elusive, that having dreams does not ensure their fulfillment. Yet often enough in these stories the protagonists are allowed the happiness and goodness they so long for, leaving room for the belief that at least sometimes things can turn out for the best.

The Chinese vision of human experience presented in this section, while drawing from a long, reflective tradition, is less inherently tragic than that of the Greeks and, in general, of the West. For while Westerners may all too often (to borrow a line from Dylan Thomas) "rage against the dying of the light," the Chinese seldom show such intensity while facing the inevitable. The Chinese believe—as the Buddha taught—that sorrow and joy are only alternate faces of reality. There are no Antigones or Medeas in these pages, though there is, in a uniquely subtle Chinese way, a full range of human experience.

Human Nature

The stories in this section evoke images of humility, honesty, self-sacrifice, compassion, foolishness, greed, and humor. While not all of the tales presented here provide these qualities in the same proportions, they do all point to the variety and richness of the human experience. These stories remind us that the aspects of human behavior that we most admire and discourage still exist—and perhaps for this reason these tales still retain much of their moral force.

Here you will find stories from an earlier, less complex age, a time when honesty and kindness were their own rewards, as well as stories telling of human folly resulting from greed. In this section you will also find stories that, though they are from "long ago and far away," will make you laugh. If these stories have anything in common, it is that they highlight, some with a touch of humor, others with irony or compassion, our shared humanity. And finally, these stories remind us to remain open to the wisdom of others.

* * *

The folktales in this volume will, I hope, provide a window into an ancient and intriguing culture, its people, and its ideas. Gathering these stories has been a humbling yet exhilarating experience for me. I hope that reading and listening to them will be equally meaningful for you.

Dragon Tales

The Legend of the Two Islands

as told by
Lu Bin

I am from the seaside city of Yingkou in southwestern Liaoning Province. The Liaohe River flows through the city, which is located on two islands. An ancient fort stands in the western part of town.

There is a legend about my hometown that I will now tell. This story is well known in Yingkou, and I have often heard elderly people tell it.

*L*ong, long ago, most of the earth was covered with ocean, including the area of my hometown. Thousands of years passed, and finally humans appeared on earth. A few people, my ancestors, came to live on islands near the area where my hometown lies now. As the oceans gradually receded, these islands became bigger and bigger. In those days, the people who lived on the islands were happy and worked hard every day. They got along well with one another, as if they were one big family.

But as often happens, good things do not last forever, and some suffering is inevitable. One day a heavy rainstorm fell on the island, lasting for seven days. Then a huge dragon appeared in the sky. He said he was the king of the sea and that the people of the islands had disturbed his peaceful life. Angry, he ordered all of the inhabitants to leave the islands within three days or they would all be killed. They were anxious and distressed because they knew they wouldn't be able to find another island to live on in just three days. The only thing they could do was to stay and try to fight the dragon.

After an evening's discussion, the townspeople came up with a plan. Two brave young men would attempt to kill the dragon the following morning. These two men would pretend to present the dragon with some treasure as a gift, then kill him while he was least suspecting an attack. The two young men knew that their chances of killing the dragon were slim but that destroying him was their only chance of saving their town from destruction.

The following morning, the huge dragon appeared once again and ordered the townspeople to leave immediately. The two young men, planning to trick the dragon, responded that he should hold off driving the townspeople away for at least a little while, because they had a wonderful treasure to present to him. The dragon, who was greedy as well as fierce, came down to one of the islands to inspect the treasure that was waiting for him. When the dragon came to the large stone on which the young men were standing, they quickly drew their swords, which they had hidden under their clothes, and stabbed the dragon in the belly. Startled and injured, the dragon took to the air, dragging the two young men into the sky with him. The great dragon rocked back and forth as he flew, in an effort to rid himself of the two men, who were holding on for dear life. Clinging to the dragon's underside, the men managed to climb onto the dragon's back. One fellow violently stabbed the dragon, trying to get at his heart, while

*I*t was summer and the peasants were working in the fields. Furious, dark clouds suddenly covered the sky, like wild horses running on the plain. The wind blew very hard, and branches swung from side to side. The peasants hurried home to shut their doors tightly.

It was so inky black that nothing could be seen. People looked out their windows in surprise. It rained heavily. Thunder sounded as if it would deafen their ears; lightning flashed as though it would blind them. To the peasants' surprise, they saw something enormous fall down to the ground from the heavens as the lightning flashed, then they heard a loud thud as it landed. It rained hard for another hour, then gradually the sky began to clear. Eventually the rain stopped. A beautiful rainbow appeared, and the sun came out from behind the clouds. Everything looked fresh, and men, women, and children went outdoors again.

The peasants were very surprised to find a big new pond near the road with a very large animal lying in it. It had long, thick hair on either side of its mouth and a head like a horse's, but much bigger. It also had a pair of huge antlers. Its body was more than one hundred meters long, covered with thousands of fishlike scales, each more than one meter in diameter. The creature had four large talons shaped like a rooster's, as well as a long tail.

An old man recognized the creature as a dragon who was in charge of rain. There are many kinds of dragons, and they all have different jobs. Some are in charge of fire, some of rain, some of sand, and so on. They are all ruled by the Emperor of Heaven and live in the seas, rivers, lakes, and even wells. At times they fly above the clouds, or even change form into people or other animals. Of course, dragons have magnificent palaces in the water. In ancient times, emperors of China regarded themselves as descendants of dragons. This was a sign of absolute power. Many temples were built to honor the dragon, and when it was dry people would pray to dragons for rain.

This dragon was dying. The people realized that he must have committed a serious crime against the Emperor of Heaven and had been punished by being hurled down to earth by the Emperor's troops. That is to say, the Emperor had taken back the dragon's supernatural powers. The people pitied the dragon from the bottom of their hearts. They felt that they must help him get back to heaven. Wasting no time, they knit a big mat of dried reeds and covered the dragon with it to prevent the sun from burning him. Then they went back to the village. Two men were left to take care of the dragon. One of the old men told the villagers to make preparations to send the dragon off, so they beat drums, blew horns, burned spices, and prayed to the Emperor of Heaven to allow the dragon to go back.

The villagers did this for nearly three days. On the third day a thick fog filled the village. As the day passed, the fog became thicker and thicker, so thick that people could not see each other. When the fog finally disappeared, several villagers ran to see the dragon but found that it had vanished. All of the townspeople gathered around the pond in astonishment. The new pond remained but the dragon was gone. It was a real miracle, and the people cheered.

As the years went by, the villagers found that the pond was never dry, even when the rains did not come. Moreover, the pond was rich in fish, shrimp, and crab. To memorialize this strange event, the villagers of Dashiqiao call this place Dragon Pond.

Land and Sea

as told by
Zhao Xing

I am from the town of Xingcheng in Liaoning Province. My hometown is quite old. It was built during the Ming Dynasty about five hundred years ago, and the ancient city wall is still well preserved. Xingcheng lies by the sea, on a beautiful curved beach from which you can see Chrysanthemum Island just offshore. We also have a hill and a hot spring, which is used to cure certain kinds of ailments.

My story is a folktale from my hometown. Everyone knows this tale because it describes how certain geographical features in Xingcheng were formed.

*O*nce upon a time there was a village by the sea in northeast China, my hometown. People made their living by fishing and growing crops. The villagers were very kind to one another, often sharing their troubles together. The climate was very good, so people had a happy and quiet life.

This life did not continue long, however, for a lazy and cruel dragon came to the village. He asked for food from the villagers instead of looking for it himself. If the dragon was not satisfied with what he received, he would destroy houses and eat farm animals or even children. The townspeople hated the dragon so much they tried to kill him, but this only caused him to take revenge on the town. Because they could not kill the dragon, the villagers had to endure him.

There was a girl in the village named Jiuhua, which means "chrysanthemum." Her boyfriend was a very brave young fellow named Shoushan. They loved each other deeply. The day before their wedding, the dragon sank a boat that was carrying both of their fathers. The couple were very sorrowful and made up their minds to kill the dragon. Early the next morning they set out to look for the dragon in spite of the villagers' pleas to leave the dragon alone.

Jiuhua and Shoushan overcame many difficulties and at last found the cave in which the dragon lived. At midnight they crept into the cave. The dragon was asleep, so the young fellow stabbed his sword into the dragon's belly. The dragon woke up in pain. Enraged, he opened his gaping mouth to bite Shoushan. When Jiuhua saw what the dragon was about to do, she threw herself onto the dragon's neck to distract him.

Finally, the wounded dragon could no longer stand the pain. He shot out of the cave, running as fast as he could. He flew into the sky to try to get rid of the couple, who were now hanging onto his back. They held the dragon's body tightly as he racked his brains to figure out how to get free of the couple. Finally, the dragon dove deep into the ocean hoping to drown them. They knew they could not survive long underwater, but still they hung on. On the seventh day the dragon died, but the couple had already been dead for days. Even after they died, they still clung tightly to the dragon. Eventually the dragon turned into a freshwater spring, the girl into an island, and the young man into a hill watching the island from across the land.

Three Mountains and a River

as told by
Chen Lihua

I live in a small town near the coastal city of Hangzhou, in Zhejiang Province. The Qiantang River in Hangzhou is very famous for the big wave that forms on it once a year. The river's entrance at the East China Sea is far wider than the rest of the river, so when the tide surges in, the river rises as it moves along. On August 15 of the lunar calendar, the tidal wave is especially large because of the position of the moon. Many people go to see the wave that day, and the event has become very well known in China. There is an interesting story about the wave and the Qiantang River that I would like to tell. This story is known by most of the people in Zhejiang Province.

*L*ong, long ago, there was a dragon king who lived under the Qiantang River. He was the ruler of all the creatures living in the sea, and he had a son who was a green dragon, as well as a very old tortoise as a helper.

These dragons had magical powers, of course, so every year on August 15 of the lunar calendar, the old dragon and his son would make the river angry. The water would surge over the bank, destroying houses and flooding the fields. At the same time, the dragons would ride a beautiful wagon on the surge, watching the people suffer from the flood. As the dragons did this they were very happy because of the people's misery. The people hated them, but nothing could be done.

At that time there happened to be a white tiger sleeping near the river. This was not a normal tiger, but a magical one who had slept for hundreds of years. When the cries of the people finally awakened him, he became very angry. "How can that old fellow do that!" he shouted. Wanting to punish the dragon, he waited near the river until the day of the surge.

Finally the day came, but this time only the young dragon and the old tortoise rode the wave happily while the people were crying and moaning. With anger in his eyes, the white tiger arched his back and jumped into the river just in front of the dragon. The dragon's horses stopped suddenly, causing the dragon to nearly fall off his wagon.

"Who are you?" the dragon shouted. "How dare you do this to me?"

The tiger in turn shouted angrily, "You needn't ask that!"

"You—you get out of my way! Do you know who I am? I'm the son of the dragon king."

"Yes, I know," replied the tiger. "You are the one I've come to kill."

The tiger lunged at the dragon and a fight began. They fought day after day, neither able to gain the advantage over the other. Eventually the dragon began to tire. As the dragon weakened, the tortoise bit the tiger's tail, causing the tiger to lose strength. The dragon once again became strong while the tiger started to lose the battle.

At that critical moment, a demigod named Lu Dongbing happened to come across the dragon and the tiger fighting. Wondering what was happening, he asked a passerby to explain. Wanting to help the people get rid of the dragon, Lu Dongbing heaved his sword into the air, which struck the dragon on the head and killed him. The great creature fell to the ground and turned into a mountain—Green Dragon

民间故事

Love

*M*any years ago in Shenyang there was a castle in an old kingdom. In the castle there lived a beautiful young lady. She had long, dark hair and big, beautiful eyes. She was kind and warm-hearted. Her father was a general who commanded many soldiers.

One fine day the young lady went out on her horse. Suddenly a carriage passed and startled her horse, who bolted wildly away from the castle. A young man appeared and restrained the horse, but not before being slightly hurt by the animal. The woman invited the man to the castle to rest. They got to know one another and soon fell in love. They were both kind, the lady was beautiful, and the man was brave.

About a year passed and the young man went to see the young lady's father to ask for his daughter's hand in marriage. The general was very surprised, then he laughed. He told the man, "How do you think you can marry my daughter? You are dreaming! You have nothing. You are poor."

The young man was not discouraged and went to the father again and again. The father became angry, telling his soldiers to take the young man to prison. The young lady heard what had happened to the young man and was saddened. Finally she killed herself. When the young man discovered what she had done, he too ended his life, unable to live without her.

Red String

as told by
Zhang Lijuan

I come from the city of Anyang, in Henan Province. Three thousand years ago Anyang was the capital of China's second oldest dynasty, the Shang. In addition to Anyang, Henan is also famous for its Luoyang peonies and for the historic Shaolin Temple.

In Henan it is the custom for young ladies to bind their pigtails with red string. It is well known that you will find a good husband if you do so! Why? The custom comes from an ancient story that I heard from my grandfather, who had many, many stories.

During the Ming Dynasty, in a village called Hujia in a mountainous area of Henan, there was a man named Hu Yuanwai. He and his wife had no sons, only one daughter named Chuiyin.

Chuiyin was young and beautiful, so beautiful that fish would sink and geese would drop from the sky when they saw her. Because of her beauty many people came every day to introduce young men to her, but her father was intent upon having her marry a high-ranking official, so her engagement was delayed. Chuiyin worried about her father's intentions for her, but she could not tell her parents. She became thinner and thinner.

One afternoon Chuiyin went into the garden alone. She saw two birds sitting in a tree, and this made her think of her own lonely existence. While walking on a small garden path, she came to a small pond and stood by it feeling very unhappy. Suddenly, she saw a young man gazing at her; her face flushed and she hurried back inside and closed the door.

The following day when she went to the garden, she again found the young man gazing at her. This time she was happy; they soon fell in love and visited with one another every day.

Not long after this, however, Chuiyin's mother found out about the girl's secret meetings. Chuiyin had to tell her mother everything. Her mother was astonished and hurried to tell the girl's father, Hu Yuanwai. Chuiyin's parents were very nervous and asked her about the young man, but she knew little about him. Finally the girl's mother suggested a way to find out more about the young man. Believing her mother's interest to be innocent, Chuiyin went along with the plan. In the evening, when the young man came again, Chuiyin pinned a needle with a long red string to his clothes.

When morning came, the girl's father followed the string into the garden with his servants. To their surprise, they found the string leading into the pond. When Hu Yuanwai tugged the string he noticed some bubbles rising to the surface of the water. Suspecting something, he ordered his servants to ladle out the water until the pond was dry. When they had finished and looked at the bottom, they found a big old tortoise lying by a large stone, the red string still pinned to his back. Hu Yuanwai immediately had the tortoise bound and burned.

That evening the young man came to Chuiyin in a dream, telling her, "Long ago, I was marshal of the East Sea. I ate a peach that the goddess had presented to the sea dragon's mother, so I was punished by being made to stay at the bottom of a pond. However, I fell in love with you, disobeying the gods, so I deserved to die. But now I worry about our son, whom you will soon bear. I wish only that you preserve my ashes and the red string. When our son grows up, look under the big stone in the pool; there you will find a large diamond. You should give him the diamond, the string, and the ashes when he takes the imperial exams. These treasures will be very useful to him." So Chuiyin saved his ashes and the string.

Soon after this dream Chuiyin had a son whom she named Biesheng. Hu Yuanwai disliked the child and had him thrown into the pond. To everyone's amazement, the child swam to safety. Chuiyin cried and shouted that she wanted to keep the child, so her father finally gave in, letting his daughter raise the boy herself.

Twenty years passed, the old couple died, and Biesheng became a handsome young man. He was very clever and studied hard. Because his mother had no income and they depended solely on their lands for food, they were poor. When the year of the imperial exam came,* Biesheng prepared for the great test. Before he left for the exam, Chuiyin was reminded of the boy's father's words in a dream, so she asked the boy to fetch the diamond from the pool. With the ashes, the red string, and the diamond, he set off on foot for the exams in the far-off capital.

One day, coming to a little village, Biesheng felt hungry and thirsty. He saw an old man by the roadside, who asked, "Are you Mr. Bie?"

The young man, quite surprised, replied, "Yes, but how do you know I'm Mr. Bie?"

Without answering Biesheng's question, the old man fell to his knees at once and said, "Mr. Bie, please save my daughter's life."

"But what must I do?" asked the young man.

The old man, whose name was Wang, explained that for several days his daughter Qiaolian had been lying unconscious from an illness. He had had a dream in which a deity spoke to him, saying, "Mr. Bie will bring your daughter back to life with his treasure. Tomorrow morning he will pass by this village. If you miss him your daughter will die."

Biesheng hurried to see Qiaolian, and, with the help of the things his mother had given him, the girl came back to life. The father was

---

* The imperial exam was given once every four years.

very grateful to Biesheng and the two young people liked one another very much, so after a short while they were engaged.

Promising to return, Biesheng continued on to the exam, where, because of his hard work, he took first place. When Biesheng returned to his home in the village of Hujia, he and his mother offered a sacrifice to his father. Biesheng and Qiaolian were married, and they lived a happy life.

To this day in Henan, young ladies like to bind their pigtails with red string so that they will find a good husband. Nowadays, whenever a man named "Bie" marries a woman named "Wang" or vice versa, it is said that their marriage will be a long and happy one.

A Sad Love Story

as told by
Shen Beilun

I live in Zhejiang Province, which is not very large but is very rich and beautiful. There are many rivers and mountains—not very high but pretty nevertheless. My hometown is Yuyao, which lies in the eastern part of the province. It is a small town with two rivers and a number of bridges, some old, some new. My hometown is a typical city for Zhejiang. The population is not very large and people work hard to earn more money so as to live a better life.

There is a beautiful but sad story from Zhejiang. I cannot remember when or where I first heard it, but it is a popular story widespread throughout the province. Almost everyone knows it, and it has been made into a play.

*L*ong, long ago, there was a beautiful girl in a small town. Her name was Zhu Yingtai. Not only was she good at sewing, but she could read and write well, which was very unusual for a Chinese woman in those days. Everyone knows that in the past Chinese women were not expected to study, much less to learn to read or write. It was believed that the less a woman knew, the better a housewife she would be. In those days, a woman was considered to be the property of her husband, and she had to rely on and obey him completely.

Zhu was not that sort of a woman. She was disgusted with the conditions she saw around her and would not obey her parents, who only hoped that she would find a suitable husband and obey him. Rather, she did what she liked and studied what she wished. At first her parents tried to prevent her from studying, but she refused to listen to them, and in the end they had to give in.

In the same town, there lived a young scholar named Liang Shanbo, whose parents were poor peasants. He loved to study, but because he was too poor to buy books, he often borrowed them from others. Liang studied hard, often staying up past midnight, and he became well known in town for his learning. In his spare time he visited friends to discuss things they had studied, and he wrote poems as well.

One night Liang went to visit a close friend of his. At his friend's house he met Zhu Yingtai. They talked for a long time that night. Zhu was attracted by Liang's abundant knowledge; he in turn was attracted by her bravery and wisdom. After that meeting, they could often be found together discussing their studies, poetry, and society. They had thorough discussions about many subjects. They did not always agree, but they always learned much from one another.

Day by day, they found that they valued each other's company. At last they fell in love and began to discuss marriage and their future. Unfortunately, Zhu Yingtai's parents objected strongly to the proposed marriage and began to prevent her from seeing Liang. They locked her in her room, but she still insisted that she be allowed to go out. At first she threw everything out of her window; when this did not work, she stopped eating. This worried her parents greatly and at last they let her out of her room. Instead of allowing her to marry Liang, however, they looked for a rich man to marry their daughter. After about a month, they found a rich family with a son who agreed to marry the girl, but the man was an ignoramus who only knew how to waste time, eat, and sleep. The man could not even write his own name.

Zhu Yingtai had no intention of obeying her parents, but this time they forced her to do what they wanted. Worst of all, Liang had gone to a big city to study and was to be gone for a long time, so even he could not help her. Because she was only a woman, and in those days women had little power, she had no way of going to look for Liang. However, she thought about him day and night, would not sleep, and had no appetite. After a few days of this torment she became ill, but her parents still insisted that she marry the man they had chosen for her.

With her own misfortunes weighing her down, Zhu Yingtai learned that Liang had gotten seriously ill due to his lack of money for proper food and lodgings. His poverty prevented him from going to a doctor; his suffering only increased when he received a letter from Zhu Yingtai describing her predicament. He worried about her constantly. Finally, lacking medicine and proper care, he died, regretting only that he could not see Zhu Yingtai before his death.

Soon death would come to Zhu Yingtai as well. At first her parents were happy about Liang's death, because they thought their daughter would stop thinking about him. They had no idea of the tragedy that would befall them. The night after she learned of Liang's death, Zhu hanged herself behind the house. Her only wish was to be buried with the body of Liang.

The next day the people of the town laid her body with Liang's and placed earth upon them. As they finished, two beautiful butterflies flew from the earth. Everyone knew that these two lovely creatures were Liang and Zhu. They had been united after all.

Many people who hear it are moved to tears. Today when a boy and a girl are dating, their parents tell them this story to let them know what love means and how to love others.

愛
情

as told by
Kang Jianjun

The Origin of Xianfei Bamboo

I come from Hunan Province, which lies in southern China, bordering Guangdong Province. Hunan's earth is rich and there is much traffic on Dongting Lake. My hometown, Yiyang, is near Dongting Lake, a body of water that is the setting for many folktales. The story I am going to tell is one of them. Near Dongting Lake, there is a place where a special kind of bamboo grows. This bamboo, called Xianfei bamboo, is covered by black spots that look like tears.

*L*ong, long ago, when Yao was emperor, the Yellow River flooded.* The land looked like an ocean; water was here and there and everywhere, and houses were underwater. Innumerable horses and cattle were carried away, and most people lost their houses and animals and were hungry and cold. Realizing how serious the problem was, the emperor ordered Da Yu** to deal with the situation. How difficult the task was! It was raining heavily, and the water was still rising. There were no tools other than spades and hands, but to save thousands of lives, Da Yu said good-bye to his wife Xianfei and left his home.

Xianfei was worried about her husband's safety, but the emperor had ordered Da Yu to help the people, so there was nothing she could do. She said good-bye to her husband with tears in her eyes, but because the task was so difficult, Da Yu had little time to think of his wife. He went at once to the flooded lands and observed firsthand the devastation caused by the river. He worked for days to get the river to flow back into the sea. He dug channels for the river, but one day he was blocked by a tall mountain holding back the water. He tried to cut through the rock, but it was too hard. Seeing this, he changed himself into a big white bear, loading the mountain into his arms and removing it. During all this time Da Yu passed his house three times, but he was so busy he did not even go in. Xianfei waited and waited but had little news of her husband. Day by day, month by month, she stood by the door looking into the road.

Several years passed and Da Yu still did not appear. Finally one day Xianfei could not bear it any longer. She ran out of the house and looked for him by the lakeside, but where was he? Only a great expanse of water like the ocean lay before her. She ran and ran, eventually becoming very tired. Near the lake at that time there grew a large stand of bamboo. Tired and sad, Xianfei leaned against the bamboo and could not help crying. She cried and cried. Her tears were like a stream flowing on the bamboo, becoming black spots that stayed on them forever. Watered by her tears, this bamboo grew up around Xianfei's house. It is said that all of the "tears" on the bamboo show how much Xianfei cried and worried for her husband.

---

* The Yellow River flows through the provinces of Henan and Shandong to the north of Hunan.

** Da Yu, or Yu the Great, is a semimythical figure said to have begun his heroic exploits in 2297 B.C. He is the first of the Yellow River's dike builders.

Spring River

as told by
Liu Zhen

I am from Tongliao, Inner Mongolia, a medium-sized city of about 600,000 people. In summer, Tongliao has many flowers. The streets are clean and wide, and pedestrians and cars pass easily through the streets. There is no industry in my city, so the air is fresh and clean.

There is a large park in my hometown named Xilamulun, which means "Spring River" in the Mongolian language. The river has disappeared, but its name has stayed as a reminder of its beauty. I want to tell you the story of this ancient salty river. This story is widely known in town. I heard it when I was a child.

*M*any years ago, there lived a Mongolian girl named Xi La Mu Lun. She was kind-hearted and beautiful. Her father was a public official. She had no brothers or sisters, and her parents loved her more than they could say. One day, when she was sixteen, she went with four servants to a temple to pay respects to the gods. On their way back, evening fell in the forest. Two servants were carrying Xi La Mu Lun on a sedan, when a strong wind suddenly began to blow. Without warning, a large tiger appeared, springing toward the girl and servants with a great roar. The girl and her servants were paralyzed with fright, and it looked as if they would all lose their lives in a moment. Just as suddenly, however, an arrow pierced the tiger's belly, causing him to turn around. The tiger faced a strong young hunter holding a large knife, who courageously killed the animal.

As the exhausted hunter wiped the sweat from his brow, Xi La Mu Lun got off her sedan to thank him for saving her life. The hunter told her that he had merely met the tiger by accident, adding, "But now it is dark, and I fear you will meet another fierce animal. May I escort you through the forest to your home?"

Xi La Mu Lun thanked him and agreed to allow him to lead them safely to her home. As they walked together, the girl learned that he lived with his mother.

When they walked out of the forest, the hunter saw them off. As he was leaving, he saw that her handkerchief had fallen out of the sedan. Examining it closely, he noticed that some words were written on it. He read, "We'll meet again, in heaven above or earth below."

The hunter was puzzled. He went home and told his mother, who only smiled, saying, "Son, she fell in love with you, so she left you her handkerchief. But her father is an important man, an official. Forget that you have met her." By this time, however, her son had also fallen in love, so he ignored his mother's advice.

Anxious to see Xi La Mu Lun again, the hunter went to the official's home, but a servant would not let him in. Though the young man explained that he had an important matter to discuss with the girl's father, the servant was afraid of what his master would do if he allowed the young man to enter. Even so, the young man was determined to see the father and finally did so. When he told the girl's father of his intentions to marry Xi La Mu Lun, showing him his daughter's handkerchief, the official was shocked. Though vowing to never allow her to marry a poor hunter, he did not say so to the young man. Instead he asked him to wait while he went to speak to his wife about the issue.

As he expected, the girl's mother was against any such marriage. Upon questioning Xi La Mu Lun, her parents found out all about what had happened in the forest and how the hunter had saved their daughter's life. Though they still opposed the marriage, they knew that it was useless to forbid the girl to see the young man. The father, however, devised a way to keep them apart, telling his daughter, "I have a way to find out if this young man really loves you or if he just likes my wealth."

The father went back to the hunter and told him, "My daughter said that if you wish to marry her, you must send her a present to show your sincerity."

"I'll do my best," the hunter replied.

The father continued, "There is a mountain about 500 miles from here. On top of the mountain, there is a dragon with a big pearl on its head. If someone got the pearl and swallowed it, he would live forever. If you really love my daughter, get this pearl."

The young man vowed to return in six months with the pearl and set off immediately. The distant mountain was 15,000 feet high, covered by snow all year long, with many dangerous crevasses and cliffs. Many people had died trying to reach the summit, and not even their bodies had survived the mountain's terrible climate. Yet none of this made the hunter hesitate.

For months, the girl heard nothing about the hunter. Often she asked her parents what had become of him. At last her parents had to tell her. She was shocked, for she knew that the young man would face many dangers getting the pearl. She realized that though he was brave and strong, his chances of surviving the mountain were small. Longing for his return, she gazed sadly out the window day and night, hoping to see her hunter return.

Eight months passed, but still the young man had not returned. One day, somehow knowing that the hunter had returned, Xi La Mu Lun hurried out into the road to see him. A ragged figure moved toward her, thin and badly injured. She ran toward him. It was the hunter, and in his hands he held an enormous pearl. Exhausted and dying, he could say nothing, only smile. The journey had taken every ounce of his strength. He collapsed and died at Xi La Mu Lun's feet.

Deep sorrow struck the girl's heart. She would not eat or speak, but only lay quietly in her bed. Fearing for her life, her parents watched over her, bringing her all kinds of delicacies to eat and drink. Nothing had any effect, and she said nothing to them. One evening, she got up. Taking a small package, she left her family forever. She walked day and night towards the mountain that had caused the hunter's death. When thirsty, she drank spring water; when hungry, she ate wild fruit. Branches and thorns ripped her clothing and scraped her skin.

Finally, after reaching the foot of the mountain, she sat down and began to weep. The sky was low and dark. Birds flew as if in slow motion, crying sorrowfully as they passed her. Animals moved near her in her misery. She cried for days and nights, then lay down and died. Her salty tears formed a river, and her body turned into trees and flowers on the sides of the river.

Hearing the story of these two sincere young lovers, people loved them very much. They buried the hunter's body beside the river, and to remember the girl and her misfortune, they called the river Xilamu-lun. In former times, people would often go there to sing songs or to place earth on the hunter's tomb.

爱情

as told by
Zhang Ling

Mo Chou Woman

*I*come from Nanjing, Jiangsu, in south-east China. Jiangsu is a fertile area called "the place full of fish and rice." It has green hills and clear lakes. Many of its cities are near water and are well known, such as Nanjing, Suzhou, and Wuxi.

In Nanjing there is a stone statue of a young lady named Mo Chou Woman. She is tall, thin, beautiful, and gentle, but she is blind. There is also a lake named after her. How was she blinded, and why is she famous throughout China? Let me tell you this story, which I learned from a teacher.

*L*ong, long ago, there lived a young girl whose name was Mo Chou. In English, this means "without worry." Mo Chou was always happy even though she lived a hard life. Her parents died when she was young, and she lived with her old, weak grandmother. Every day she had plenty of work to do, such as cooking, sewing, washing, sweeping the floor, and so on. As young as she was, she had to plant crops in the fields like a strong adult man. She had neither enough food to eat nor good clothes to wear, but she was beautiful and clever, and even people far from town knew about her.

In a village about ten li from her home, there lived a young man named Jiao Ping, who was handsome and wealthy, and, though he was born to a large, rich family, he was very kind. He had heard about Mo Chou for some time but never had a chance to see her. One day while he was at the market, he saw a beautiful young lady; learning from his servant that this was Mo Chou, he fell deeply in love with her immediately.

When he got home that day, he told his mother he wanted to marry Mo Chou. His mother became very angry, saying that while Mo Chou was humble and respectable, he could not marry such a poor girl. The young man insisted that if he could not marry Mo Chou he would not marry anyone. His mother had no choice but to give in. Shortly after this the girl's grandmother died, so Mo Chou was even more alone than before. Considering these circumstances, before long they were married.

After she became the wife of Jiao Ping, Mo Chou worked even harder than before to satisfy his family. She was a good daughter-in-law indeed, but her mother-in-law was never satisfied with her. In the mother-in-law's eyes, everything Mo Chou did was incorrect or badly done. She dropped the food the girl cooked and threw away the clothes she sewed. She was very cruel to Mo Chou, making her work day and night, even abusing her with rough words and beating her. Though Jiao Ping loved his wife deeply, he worked in another town far away and seldom came home, so he could not control what happened there. Mo Chou endured this torment alone; now she was no longer "without sorrow" as her name implied. She would have preferred her earlier life alone, but she could do nothing to make her situation better. Not wanting to cause trouble, when her husband came home she pretended to be happy, lest Jiao Ping argue with his mother.

One cold winter morning, Mo Chou had a high fever and got up a bit later than usual. Of course, her mother-in-law beat her bitterly; hungry, cold, and weak, Mo Chou was thrown to the snowy ground. Jiao Ping happened to return home that evening and found Mo Chou black and blue all over. Enraged, he accused his mother of mistreating his wife. During their violent argument, his mother attacked Mo Chou, poking her eyes with large needles and blinding her. Blood rushed from Mo Chou's eyes and she felt bitter pain. When she realized what had happened to her, she bolted out of the house so quickly that Jiao Ping could not catch her. She ran straight to the lake near the house and jumped in. Though Jiao Ping raced after her, he could not stop her. He jumped into the lake too, crying "Mo Chou, I'm coming!"

Neither of their bodies was ever found. In memory of this unfortunate girl the lake is called Mo Chou Lake.

爱情

as told by
Xiao Jun

Shennu Peak

The Yangtze is a very famous river in China. Not only is it the longest river in the country, but it is also very important for commerce and transportation. My hometown, the city of Wanxian, is located on the banks of the Yangtze in Sichuan Province. Each year many tourists visit my hometown to enjoy the beautiful scenery of the Three Gorges near Wanxian. When I was a child, old people often told me this story about Shennu Peak. Some people cry when they hear it.

*L*ong, long ago, there stood a small village beside the Yangtze. People in the village lived a hard but peaceful life. The men went fishing and the women kept the houses. In the village, there was a young man named Anhu and a young woman named Ahua. They fell in love and soon were married. They loved each other deeply. Each day Anhu went to the Yangtze and returned in the evening with many fish. While Anhu fished, Ahua cleaned the house and did the cooking, and they lived very happily. This good situation, however, did not last long.

One morning Anhu went out as usual, not noticing the dark clouds in the sky. After he said good-bye to Ahua, he rowed his little boat to the middle of the river where he began to fish. Several hours later the wind began to blow, and Anhu realized that a big storm was coming. Though he rowed fast and hard, he could not bring his small boat to shore. The wind blew harder and harder. Suddenly a large wave tipped Anhu and his boat over, and poor Anhu was drowned.

In the evening Anhu did not come home as usual, so Ahua became anxious. She climbed a rock to look down at the Yangtze, but she saw nothing. "Could something have happened to Anhu?" she wondered, trying to reassure herself that nothing was wrong. She waited and waited, and still Anhu did not return. She waited for many days, and at last she turned into a rock, which people called Beauty Peak, and later Shennu Peak. Today Shennu Peak stands as a reminder of Ahua's sorrowful wait for Anhu.

爱
情

as told by
Mei Zhe

Qinghai Lake

The province of Qinghai lies on the Qin-zang Plateau, and the weather there is worse than in most other places in China. Its economy depends mainly on agriculture and raising animals. Cows and sheep are seen here and there on the grasslands. Qinghai's most famous places are Qinghai Lake, the largest saltwater lake in China, and Ta Er, an important Tibetan monastery. The capital of Qinghai is Xining.

One hundred forty miles from Xining, there is a beautiful lake called Qinghai, which is surrounded by grasslands. The people who live near the lake refer to it as "the tears of a girl." There is a sad story, well known to the people of the region, about how the lake got this name.

*L*ong, long ago, a poor shepherd boy lived in Qinghai. His name was Lazhan and he was an orphan. After his parents died he made his living by tending sheep for others. When he grew up he became a handsome young man. One day, while he was tending his sheep on the grasslands, he saw a girl on the riverbank. She was a beautiful girl with long hair and a pair of bright eyes. She seemed to be weighed down by many sad matters, so Lazhan approached and asked her what was wrong. The girl did not tell him and went away.

The next day Lazhan saw her again in the same place, but she would not talk to him. Again she went away. This went on day after day. Though the girl remained quiet, Lazhan always talked to her and offered to help her with her troubles. At last the girl was moved by Lazhan's kindness. She told him that her name was Zhuoma and that she was the granddaughter of the Queen of Heaven. She said that she preferred to live on earth rather than in heaven, and for this reason she sneaked away from her mother's heavenly palace to spend time in the world of men and women. Now she did not want to return, but she did not know where to go.

After hearing this, Lazhan fell in love with her, inviting her to his home. Zhuoma thought and thought, because she knew she was forbidden to marry a mortal. She finally agreed to go with Lazhan because she loved him. Soon they were married and lived a happy life on earth. During the day she would go with Lazhan to tend the sheep, where he would tell her stories and she would sing to him. At night they would lie in the grasslands whispering softly to one another. Zhuoma told Lazhan of life in the heavenly palace, how it was dull and boring. She hated life there and preferred the life of men and women.

Despite her happiness, Zhuoma feared her grandmother would send someone to carry her back to heaven. In time she became very scared. Lazhan embraced her and promised to protect her. It is said that one year on earth equals one day in heaven, so after Zhuoma and Lazhan had been married for five years, the immortals in heaven discovered that Zhuoma was missing from the palace. The queen became very angry and sent one of her servants to take Zhuoma home. When he arrived at her house she did not want to go, telling him angrily that she would die before leaving her husband.

As the man turned to leave, he asked whether she realized the punishment she would receive for disobeying her grandmother. She answered that she did. At this the man began to walk away, turning after a short distance to throw a smoking box at Zhuoma. She fell to the ground.

When Lazhan returned in the evening, he found his wife lying on the floor. She opened her eyes slowly, crying, "I am dying. My grandmother sent someone to punish me." Lazhan wept out of anger and grief and told Zhuoma he would save her. She shook her head sadly, saying that nothing could save her except a certain kind of flower that grew on a far-off snowy mountain, a flower that no one had ever found.

Lazhan laid her on her bed and said firmly, "I must save you. I will get this flower, only you must wait for me."

Then he turned and left his wife to hunt for this rare and difficult-to-find flower. Time passed quickly and soon a month had gone by, but still Lazhan had not returned. One day, as Zhuoma was lying in bed, a neighbor came and told her that Lazhan had died. Zhuoma wept, swearing in her wretchedness to find her husband even if she died while trying. So she climbed mountain after mountain in search of her husband, but found no one.

Lazhan, however, had not died. He returned home with the flower that could save his wife, only to find that she was not there. Hearing that she had left in search of him, he set out again. He found her a long way from home just as she was dying. When Zhuoma saw Lazhan she did not say a word. Tears flowed from her eyes, then she died. It is said that her body changed into a lake, Qinghai Lake, and that the water in the lake today is from the tears of poor Zhuoma.

爱情

as told by
Dai Dongdong

Shepherd Girl

I come from Longxi County in Gansu Province. There are many historic places in Gansu, such as the rock caves in Dunhuang, the Silk Road, and Jiayuguang—the end of the Great Wall. There are also many folktales about these places. My hometown is a small town with many mountains around it. A large gate-tower stands in the center of town. It is said that this tower was once part of an important military fort in ancient times.

When you walk into my hometown you will see a tall statue of a slim, beautiful shepherd girl, with many sheep around her. The story I will tell is about her. Though I heard this story from an elderly man, nearly everyone in town knows this folktale.

*L*ong, long ago, there was a dragon king who lived in our region. He was very powerful and ruled over the sea. He had a very beautiful, kind daughter who was married to a rich man. At first her husband treated her well, though later he began to lose interest in her and even to beat her. Finally he drove her away. She suffered greatly as a result of this cruel and unfair treatment. In the winter she had to endure the piercing cold wind, shivering in the heavy snow. In the summer the scorching sun blazed down upon her like fire, burning her skin. Despite all her suffering, she had no one to talk to except the sheep she had begun to keep. How eager she was to return to her parents! But she had no way to let them know where she was and what misfortunes had befallen her.

Seldom did anyone pass by to greet her or to stop and talk. One day, however, as she was tending her flock in the cold wind, a handsome young man passed by and saw the poor girl. This young man was a clever and promising student, though from a poor family. His name was Li Ao and he was on his way to take part in the annual exams that were held all around China in those days. When he saw the poor girl he felt great pity for her, asking, "Why are you all alone? Where is your home? Where is your husband?"

Hearing this, the girl could not help crying. She told him what had happened to her and how she had suffered because of her cruel husband. Li Ao was deeply moved and asked her if there was anything he could do to help her.

She told him, "I have a hair clasp and a letter. Please take them to the ocean. There you will find a large tree on the shore, which you must tap three times. A man will rise from the ocean to meet you. Pass the clasp to him and he will take you to the bottom of the sea, where my parents live. Please give this clasp and this letter to them."

The shepherd girl took the hair clasp and the letter from her pocket and gave them to Li Ao, thanking him for his kindness. Several days later Li Ao finished his exams and went to the sea as he had promised. He knocked on the tree as the girl had told him to do, and soon a soldier with a sword appeared from the water. Li Ao gave the hair clasp to the soldier, who took him deep into the sea to a splendid palace with many treasures and colorful lights. There were several people dining with the dragon king, and everyone looked delightful. Li Ao was taken before the king and queen, and he passed the letter and the hair clasp to the king, telling him, "Your daughter asked me to give these to you. She has suffered much." Reading the letter, the king learned of his daughter's misfortunes, and both he and the queen were greatly grieved by their daughter's pain. The king wasted no time in ordering his soldiers to rescue his daughter and bring her to his palace.

After returning home to her father's palace, the girl began a new life, leaving her sorrows behind her. Though she was again a beautiful princess, she could not forget the poverty and suffering she had experienced. She was haunted even more by the memory of the handsome young man who had helped her, for she had fallen in love with him. The young man, by the way, had placed first in the exams and had become an important government official. When the king found out that his daughter had fallen in love with Li Ao, he sent someone to tell him. This story ends happily—can you guess how? Li Ao and the princess married and lived happily ever after.

The Lovers from Two Warring Tribes

as told by
Zhang Kai

I am from Liaoyang, in Liaoning Province. The seasons are beautiful here. In the spring, the trees and grasses turn green and all kinds of flowers bloom. People make kites and send them flying into the sky. In the summer, it is very hot, so the best thing to do is to swim. During late summer, there are many fruits and vegetables, such as apples, pears, tomatoes, and potatoes. In the autumn, the leaves turn gold and begin to fall. Peasants are very busy at this time of year. In the winter, the weather turns very cold, and people wear thick clothes to keep them warm. It often snows; the whole world turns white, and children can be seen making snowmen.

Here is an instructive story I heard from my grandmother when I was six years old.

*M*any years ago, there were two tribes in Liaoyang. There was a long-standing feud between these two peoples, and many people were killed in the battles. A youngster, the son of the chief of one of the tribes, was very brave. By and by, his bravery won a lot of girls' hearts, but he never fell in love with any of them. In his dreams, however, he saw a beautiful snow-white princess with a pair of bright eyes and long hair, a sweet face and red lips.

One day when he went out to hunt by a nearby lake, he heard singing like a bird in spring. Following the voice toward the lake, he saw something he had never seen before. A beautiful girl and her maids were bathing and singing by the water. To his amazement, he saw that she was the girl he had often seen in his dreams. He fell in love with her at once.

Though the boy wanted very much to talk to the girl, he did not want to approach while they were bathing. He moved some distance away from the lake and waited until they were finished, then walked towards the lake. When he appeared in front of the princess, she was instantly attracted to him. From then on they frequently met at the lake. They soon discovered that they were from the warring tribes. Because the girl was the daughter of the chief of the other tribe, it was impossible for them to marry, though they loved each other very much. They felt bitterly about this, but there was nothing they could do, as their tribes were still fighting one another.

A year later the girl discovered that she was going to have a baby, though she did not dare tell her father. To hide the truth, she told her father that while she was swimming, a lovely bird flew over her head and laid an egg, which she happened to swallow. After some days she discovered that she had a baby growing inside her. Though her story was strange her father believed her, and some months later she bore a chubby, white baby boy, who quickly became the apple of his mother's eye.

As the years passed, the boy grew more and more handsome, as well as clever and brave. Because of the story his daughter had told him, the girl's father truly believed that the boy was the son of one of the gods. He gave the boy a good education and excellent training, so when he grew up he became a powerful warrior. The son eventually united the two warring tribes and even went on to found a new dynasty, the Qing. His descendants ruled China for more than two hundred years.

爱情

as told by
Ma Ming

Lunan Henge

I am from Chengjian, in Yunnan Province. One of the most interesting attractions near my hometown is a natural formation called Lunan Henge, consisting of many grotesque stones in unusual shapes. Among the stones, one is the most famous. It is called Arshima, which was a girl's name long ago. Arshima has stood for many, many years with watchful eyes looking tranquilly to the north. Her pensive gaze seems to reveal her sad love story. Every year, thousands of people come to Lunan Henge and listen to the intriguing story of Arshima. While there are several tales about her, this one was told by one of my friends when we were children.

A long time ago, there was a poor family who lived in the small village of Lunan. The poor family had a son named Aryong, an industrious, kind-hearted, and handsome fellow. His neighbors had a beautiful daughter named Arshima. She was intelligent and charming. Although she did not have any exquisite clothes or ornaments, she was so beautiful that people would stop and stare at her. Aryong and Arshima played together when they were young, and after they grew up they fell in love with one another.

In the village, there lived another family that was very rich. They had a son called Argou. Argou idled about and did no decent work all day. He coveted Arshima's beauty and had an unquenchable desire to marry her. Time passed quickly, and Aryong and Arshima prepared to marry in the autumn, when they were twenty years old. This, however, made Argou very unhappy, for he wanted Arshima to be his bride. Argou searched for a way to take Arshima for himself. Hearing that laborers were needed to build a reservoir in the north, Argou bribed the local governor to have Aryong registered among the workers needed for the project, despite his marriage in just a few weeks.

Aryong and Arshima had no alternative, so they decided to postpone their wedding for a year until Aryong came back. With tears in her eyes, Arshima saw her beloved fiancé off at the border of their small village. Having made solemn pledges of love, they reluctantly said good-bye to each other. After Aryong left, Argou courted Arshima. Although he made many promises to be good to Arshima and her family and gave her many treasures as dowries, Arshima continually rebuffed Argou.

Seeing that riches could not move Arshima at all, Argou changed his tactics. He found fault with Arshima and her parents; even worse, he threatened to kill her entire family. Yet all of this failed, for Arshima's love for Aryong could not be altered. Argou's failure to win Arshima angered him even more, and an evil idea occurred to Argou. He sent a bribe to the overseer of the reservoir construction project on which Aryong was working. Supplies were reduced and the overseer found fault with Aryong, who became ill because of the poor conditions. He was allowed no rest and was punished severely. Aryong died on the eve of his return to Arshima.

Tidings of Aryong's death arrived at the village. Deeply sorrowful, Arshima went to the end of the small village where they had made their solemn pledges of love and stood there with wistful eyes looking to the north. Her sad gaze seemed to tell people her sorrowful story and condemn the injustices of the world. She stood there tranquilly for forty-nine days, gradually becoming stone. Arshima's loyalty in love moved the God in Heaven. So that Arshima would not feel lonely, he made many other natural stone statues to stand by her side.

as told by
Jia Jie

River Snail Girl

My hometown is Shanghai, a name many people are familiar with. Shanghai is a world-famous city, and it is also the largest city in China. Shanghai lies in the eastern part of China and faces the sea, so it is a major seaport. There is the Huangpu River in Shanghai, which runs across the city from west to east, then flows into the sea. Because of Shanghai's position at the mouth of the Yangtze River, the city's industries and manufacturers have developed very quickly. In recent years, many tall buildings have been constructed, and quite a few trees and flowers have been planted.

The city of Shanghai is not only a modern city, but it also has many folktales. I will tell you one I heard from my grandmother when I was a child.

*O*nce upon a time, when Shanghai was only a small fishing village, there lived a poor young man named Aming whose parents had died when he was a child. Aming lived alone in the village facing the sea. Every day he went to the sea to fish to make his living. Although he was very poor, he tried his best to help whenever people asked something of him.

One day after fishing, Aming was on his way home when he caught sight of a black thing lying on the side of the road. As he approached, he saw that it was a big river snail that had somehow gotten away from the water. "This snail will surely die for lack of water if I don't take it home with me," he thought to himself.

He picked up the snail and continued on his way. As soon as he reached home, he wiped the mud off the snail's shell, then carefully placed it in a jar with water. From then on, he often changed the water so that the snail would have a clean place to live.

Several months later, one night after Aming had worked hard at the sea near his house, he suddenly saw a column of smoke rising from his chimney. He was so surprised that he ran home. When he entered the house and searched, he found no one there at all. On the table, however, there were several bowls of delicious-smelling food.

"Maybe a kind soul has come to prepare food for me. I must find and thank them," thought Aming.

Strangely, the same thing happened on the second day, then on the third, fourth, and fifth days. By this time Aming was incredulous about what was happening, so he decided to ask the villagers who had done his cooking for the past five days. To his surprise, no one admitted to making his meals. Aming decided to find out for himself.

One sunny day, Aming brought out his net and went fishing as usual. After a while, he returned home and hid outside his house. Crouching down, he peered into the window so that he could see clearly what was happening inside the house. To his great astonishment, he saw a very pretty girl cooking at the stove. The girl looked like a fairy. At the sight of her Aming rushed in and seized her by the arm. The girl was surprised and wanted to flee, but she could not because Aming held her so tightly.

"Who are you, pretty girl?" Aming asked excitedly. "Why are you helping me?"

Looking at the ground, the girl said shyly, "I'm just the river snail you saved. I found you to be a warm-hearted man and wanted to do you a favor to thank you. Would you permit me to stay here with you?" The girl's cheeks turned bright red, but this only made her more beautiful.

"Truthfully," Aming replied, "I have begun to fall in love with you, lovely girl. But I am very poor. I am an orphan and my parents died when I was still a little boy. I am afraid I am too poor to provide well for a wife."

"Honest man," the girl answered, "perhaps you have mistaken me for someone else. I love you not for your money, but for your kindness and simplicity. I want to spend my life with you, living through all of the suffering and joy that life has to offer. Do you believe me?"

"Yes," replied Aming with great joy, "you are a wonderful girl and today is the happiest day in my life."

Soon Aming and the young girl got married. After the wedding, Aming went to the sea to fish as before, and the girl stayed home. They both loved each other deeply. Aming and his lovely wife lived a happy life in their seaside village.

爱
情

as told by
Liu Bing

Can Dreams Save Lives?

Acheng, my hometown, lies in the northwest of China in Heilongjiang Province. Up until six years ago, it was a small town near the famous ice city of Harbin; now it is a thriving, developing city. Several large factories have been set up in Acheng, one of which is famous all over our country for the large profit it makes every year. In addition, Acheng has a long history. It was a battlefield between the Jin and the Song during the Song Dynasty. At that time the Jin intruded upon the Song, and their battleground is just 300 meters from my home.

The story I will tell is said to be true. These events happened during World War I.

*T*here are many old castles in southern Heilongjiang. In this region there lived a young girl in a small village who was in love with a soldier. During World War I, he had to leave her to fight against the Japanese.

Later on, the girl began to dream about him. Her first dream came about a month before the end of the war. In this dream, she saw him in a dark place among some rocks. He was trying to move some of the rocks, but he could not. He stopped trying and sat down on the ground alone in the dark. The girl had this dream several times.

The following summer, her dream changed. In the new dream, she saw a castle on a hill. Part of the castle had fallen down, and there were many stones on the ground below the broken part. She went toward these stones in her dream, and she heard the voice of her boyfriend coming from under the stones. She tried to lift some of the stones, but she was too weak to do so and had to go away sadly.

The second dream replaced the previous one, and she saw the same stones several times in her sleep on other nights. She told her mother about it, and a lot of people in the village heard about her dream, but most of them did not much care. A girl's dreams were not important to other people.

Finally the girl decided that she had to find the castle. She was quite sure that it was a real one, but there were many old castles in that part of the country, so she had few hopes of finding the one in her dreams. Her dreams continued, however, and one day she could not bear it any longer. She began a long journey on foot in search of the castle in her dreams.

Day after day, she went onward, looking for the castle. She slept on the ground beside the road, and sometimes farmers gave her something to eat. For them, her story was only another sad tale from the war, but they were kind-hearted.

One day in the spring, she came to a small town, where a castle stood on top of a hill. It was the one she had often seen in her dreams. She ran toward it, collapsing on the ground in front of the castle. A crowd gathered to listen to her story, but the people had little interest in her dream or the castle, because they saw the castle every day.

Recovering her strength, she went to the fallen stones at the bottom of the castle wall, accompanied by some of the villagers. She asked them to lift the stones, and they did so only out of curiosity at her strange request. Though they did not think that her dreams meant anything, they supposed that lifting a few stones would do no harm.

The first day the villagers found nothing, but on the second day they heard a man's voice calling from below. The girl knew the voice; it was her boyfriend. The men quickly enlarged the hole and soon were able to lift him out. The boyfriend had been in the darkness for two years, and at first the light of the sun blinded him. After some time, however, he was able to look around with surprise at the people who were standing there.

The boyfriend told the story of how he had survived underground for so long. During the war, he had entered the castle for protection, but part of the castle was hit by a bomb, trapping him. He had lived on food he had found in the castle. Only his girlfriend's dreams saved him.

What made her have these dreams? How did she know about the castle where he was trapped, a castle she had never seen? Yet her dreams saved his life.

Suddenly a boy came running from a nearby hill. "Quick, come and see." He was out of breath. "Come and see what is happening in our village," he shouted to the villagers in the fields as he ran toward them.

Xiaozhen and her friends ran to the hill. When they reached the top they saw something that made them gasp. The village looked as if it were covered with white snow, shining under the bright sunlight. Their houses were nowhere to be seen. Only the roofs of a few taller houses were still showing, and there on the roof of the farmer's house they saw the farmer waving his hands and crying for help.

"Help! Help! . . . Stop!" The hoarse voice of the greedy farmer reached the villagers.

"The rich farmer must have stolen the magic pot, and he forgot the magic words to stop it," one villager said.

"Ka-duu-duo," said Xiaozhen softly, and the pot stopped immediately.

Well, it was a long time before the villagers cleaned all the streets in the village. The children had never been so happy, for they could eat their way through it.

The rich farmer was rescued by the villagers. He had learned his lesson. Whenever he became greedy again, the villagers only had to ask him, "Would you care for a bowl of nice creamy porridge?" and he would turn pale and behave himself.

as told by
Zhang Dongdong

The Boy with the Magic Brush

I was born in Fushun, which lies in the eastern part of Liaoning Province. Before World War II Fushun was called the Coal Capital, but during the war the Japanese mined most of the coal, so now the city is known more for its oil industry.

Fushun is of historical interest, for the Qing Dynasty began there. In addition, Fushun has a well-known dam where you can swim and climb a nearby hill. Close by are forests for recreation and walking.

When I was a child, my grandmother told me lots of stories and folktales. My favorite was called "The Boy with the Magic Brush." Now I will tell it to you.

*O*nce upon a time, in a little village, a poor boy named Ma Liang was born. It was not long before both his parents died, so he became an orphan. To survive he had to work for a landlord. He worked day and night.

One day, after finishing his work, he returned to his shabby bed in his shabby little house. When he passed the window of the landlord's house, he saw an artist drawing a picture for the landlord. What a beautiful scene it was! Ma Liang admired it very much. He wanted so much to have a brush to draw with.

"Would you give me a brush to draw?" he asked the landlord.

"You? Ha!" replied the landlord. "A beggar wanting to draw! Are you joking?"

At this, everyone present laughed at Ma Liang. This made him so angry that he made up his mind then and there to learn how to draw. And he vowed to draw only for the poor.

From then on, he began to practice drawing. Whatever he saw and wherever he was, he drew. Because he had no brush, he used a branch or whatever else he could get his hands on. He had no paper, so he often drew in the sand.

Years went by and Ma Liang became a good artist. Everything he drew was as lovely as if it were real. He only wished he had a brush!

One night, after practicing drawing, he went to bed. Because he was so tired he began to dream very quickly. Suddenly he was in a different place. A brook led off into the distance with all kinds of flowers on both banks, and an old man stood in front of him. Ma Liang was too surprised to say a word!

"You want your own brush, don't you?" the old man asked.

"Yes, I do!" replied Ma Liang.

"Well then, I will give you a brush. But remember that you promised to draw only for the poor." With this, the old man disappeared.

"But where is the brush?" Ma Liang wondered anxiously. "Where?"

When Ma Liang awoke he realized that it had only been a dream, but to his surprise there was a real brush in his bed. He was very pleased. The first thing he did was to draw a cock on the wall. No sooner had he finished the drawing than the cock stepped out of the wall and came to life. Ma Liang had received a magic brush!

Ma Liang began to draw for the poor. Because he could draw whatever he wanted and whatever he drew came to life, he did a lot of good with his brush. It was not long before the emperor heard the news and ordered his soldiers to bring Ma Liang to him.

The emperor met Ma Liang in his big hall. The emperor said, "I have heard that you have a magic brush that can bring whatever you draw to life. Is this true?"

"Yes," replied Ma Liang.

"Then give it to me," ordered the emperor.

"No. It's mine," responded Ma Liang.

"How dare you say that?" fumed the emperor. "I am the emperor. You must obey me. Now give it to me!" At this, two guards snatched the brush from Ma Liang's hands.

The emperor put the brush into the hands of the most respected painter in the kingdom and asked him to draw something, but his painting did not become real. Seeing that his plan was not working, the emperor tried to persuade Ma Liang to draw something. Ma Liang, however, decided to teach the emperor a lesson.

"What would you like me to draw for you?" asked Ma Liang.

"Gold. A hill made of gold," replied the emperor.

Ma Liang began to draw, not a hill of gold, but a picture of the ocean.

"Fool, I want gold!" roared the emperor.

So Ma Liang drew an island of gold in the ocean. "Now draw a ship," ordered the emperor. A ship soon appeared in the picture. The emperor hurriedly jumped into the ship with his guards and prime minister to set sail for the island of gold. The ship sat quietly, so the emperor once again ordered Ma Liang to draw, this time wind so that the ship could move.

Ma Liang wasted no time in drawing a violent wind that almost capsized the ship. The emperor screamed for Ma Liang to stop, but Ma Liang only drew more and more bad weather until the ship disappeared out of sight.

Ma Liang continued drawing for the poor. Both he and the poor were happy.

魔术

as told by
Wenshi Hao

The Magic Kettle

I am from the town of Ningdu in Jiangxi Province. My home province lies in the southern part of China, and its capital city is Nanchang. The largest body of water in China, Poyang Lake, lies in Jiangxi Province, as does Lushan Mountain. Both are famous places for tourists to visit. Tea and oranges are plentiful, and agriculture is more important than industry in my region. The following happened in the Ming Dynasty. I heard this story from my friend's grandfather in my hometown.

*I*n the middle of Jiangxi Province, high in the mountains, an old man lived in his little wooden house. He was very proud of his home and never tired of admiring the whiteness of his straw and the pretty wooden walls, which in warm weather allowed the fragrance of the trees and flowers to come in.

One day he stood looking at the mountains when he heard a rumbling noise in the room behind him. He turned around and in the corner he saw a rusty old iron kettle, which could not have seen the light of day for many years. The old man did not know how the kettle got there. He cleaned off the dust and took it into the kitchen, saying with a smile, "That was luck. A good kettle costs money. My other kettle is nearly worn out now." He took the old kettle off the fire, then filled the new one with water and put it on the fire.

No sooner was the water getting warm when a strange thing happened. The man, standing nearby, thought he must be dreaming. First the handle of the kettle gradually changed its shape and became a head. Out of the body sprang four paws, and in a few minutes the man found himself watching not a kettle, but a fox.

The fox jumped off the fire and bounded about the room like a cat, running up the walls and over the ceiling. The old man was afraid. He cried to a neighbor for help, and the two of them managed to catch the fox and shut it up safely in a wooden box. Then, quite exhausted, they sat down and talked about what they should do with this troublesome little beast. At last they decided to sell it and asked a child passing by to send them a certain tradesman named Wang.

When Wang arrived, the old man told him he had something that he wanted to get rid of, and he lifted the lid of the wooden box. To the old man's surprise, no fox was inside, only the old kettle. It was certainly very strange, but the man remembered what had taken place on the fire and did not want to keep the kettle in the house any longer. After a little bargaining about the price, Wang went away carrying the kettle. Wang had not gone very far before he felt the kettle getting heavier and heavier. By the time he reached home he was so tired that he was thankful to put the kettle down in the corner of his room and forget about it.

Around midnight, however, he was awakened by a loud noise in the corner where the kettle stood, so he raised himself up in bed to see what it was. Nothing was there except the kettle. He thought he must have been dreaming and fell asleep again, only to be roused a second time by the same noise. He jumped up and went to the corner, and, by the light of the lamp he always kept burning, he saw that the kettle had become a fox, which was running around chasing its tail. How should he deal with the creature? The tradesman was much troubled, and it was almost morning before he managed to get any sleep. When he opened his eyes in the morning, there was no fox, only the old kettle in the corner.

As soon as he had cleaned his house, Wang set off to tell his story to a friend. The friend listened quietly and did not appear too surprised, for in his youth he had heard something about a wonder-working kettle.

"Go and travel with it; display it," the friend suggested, "and you'll become a rich man. But be careful to ask the fox's permission. It would also be wise to perform some magic ceremonies to prevent it from running away at the sight of people."

Wang thanked his friend for his instructions, which he followed exactly. The fox agreed, so Wang built a booth and hung a notice outside inviting people to come and witness the most wonderful scene. They came in crowds and the kettle was passed from hand to hand. People were allowed to examine it all over and even to look inside. Then Wang took it back and set it on the platform, commanding it to become a fox. In an instant the handle began to change into a head and the spout into a tail, while the four paws appeared at the sides.

"Dance," said Wang, and the fox did its steps. Then people could not stand still any longer and they began to dance, too. Day after day the booth was so full that it was hardly possible to enter it. Wang became a rich man, yet he did not feel happy. He was an honest man and thought he owed some of his wealth to the man from whom he had bought the kettle. One morning, he put a hundred gold pieces into the kettle, and, hanging it on his arm, he returned to the old man who had sold it to him.

"I have no right to keep this kettle any longer," he added when he had finished his story, "so I have brought it back to you. Inside you will find a hundred gold pieces I have put there as the price of its hire."

The man thanked Wang, saying that few people would have been as honest. The kettle brought them both luck. Everything went well with both men until they died, which they did when they were very old and respected by everyone.

魔术

as told by
Wang Qiu

The Strange Apple Tree

I am from a small city in Liaoning Province near Anshan and Yingkou. In my hometown, people sell a lot of clothes and leather, which are reasonably priced. Many people come to visit and buy the products sold there.

The story I will tell happened in Heilongjiang, not Liaoning. I heard this story from my grandfather, whose neighbor was from Heilongjiang.

*I*n ancient times there lived a mother and her son, a boy named Nor-man. They were very poor, and the mother made a living by weaving cloth. There was also a forest nearby. One day she went to the market to sell cloth. On her way home, she had only one penny in her hand. She was thinking about how to spend it when suddenly she saw an old woman begging beside the road. The old woman was so weak that she did not have enough strength to speak, but could only nod at her. Because the mother was also a poor woman, she felt pity for the old woman. Without giving it a second thought, she put her one penny into the old woman's hand. The old woman was grateful and said to her, "If your son mastered a skill and did good things for people, he would be happy and you would prosper." Then the old woman disappeared.

The mother went back home immediately and explained to her son what had happened, adding that he must begin soon to study a skill. Nor-man, however, did not know which skill suited him best, so he began by asking a tailor if he could learn his trade. The tailor, of course, told him that being a tailor was the best thing in the world, so Nor-man began to study how to cut, measure, and sew clothes. After only a month, however, Nor-man got bored. He told his mother, "Tailors are useful for the rich, but the poor don't have enough money to buy clothes." His mother eventually had to give in and let Nor-man quit tailoring.

One day, not long after Nor-man had given up learning to be a tailor, he passed a barber shop. He walked in and asked the barber, "Which craft is the best, sir?" The barber answered without hesitation that his craft was indeed the finest. Nor-man wasted no time in asking the barber to teach him.

A month or so later, Nor-man went home and told his mother, "I don't want to be a barber. I'm not willing to cut only the hair of proud rich people, while the poor can't afford to pay."

Nor-man's mother, quite angry this time, retorted, "What are you going to do on this earth? You don't like any of the trades you've tried, so you have no choice but to become a herdsman and tend cattle every day."

This seemed a simple way of life to Nor-man, requiring little skill, and he was quite content to spend his days caring for a herd of cattle. The cattle were gentle, and Nor-man looked after them lovingly; they became friends.

One day one of the cattle began to speak to Nor-man, telling him, "Do not be afraid. The King of Heaven has sent me here as punishment because of a mistake I made. Nevertheless, I'm very grateful that you have taken good care of me and haven't harmed me. Because you have been so kind, I will help you. If you are ever in trouble, you may grasp my ears and say 'fly.' Then you will be freed from your trouble."

One day, as Nor-man was walking along a road in the countryside, he saw heavy smoke coming from the forest nearby and realized that something was burning. Nor-man took the animal by the ears, saying, "Fly." With a jolt they both leaped into the air and sailed toward the forest. There they saw a small beetle trapped inside the fire. Wasting no time, Nor-man took a stick and put it into the fire. The beetle crawled out of the fire on the stick and at once became an old woman. She told them to follow her, leading them to a cave in a mountainside, with a heap of jewelry inside.

The old woman said, "If you choose the red jewelry, you'll be the most handsome man in the world." Then she pointed to an apple tree beside them, saying, "If you own this apple tree, you'll still be a poor man, but you'll do some good things for people, and your mother will be happy."

Nor-man told her that he wanted the apple tree. The old woman gave it to him, telling him, "Plant this tree in front of your house. It will blossom and grow fruit every day. These apples can cure many diseases, but you must not take any money for them."

Nor-man promised to do exactly as she said, then went back home with the apple tree. From that day on Nor-man, with the help of his apple tree, cured the diseases of many poor people.

Soon, however, the lord in Nor-man's village heard about the magic apple tree. He sent several of his servants to Nor-man's house, where they stole the tree and planted it in the nobleman's yard. After only a few days the tree withered and died, though no one could explain why. Nor-man became very sad because he now had no apples to cure the poor. In his mind, he went over what the old woman had told him, then he even went back to the mountain to look for her. He found her again, telling her what had happened. The old woman, however, already knew all about what the lord had done. This time, she gave Nor-man two types of apples, explaining what he should do with them.

Nor-man went back home and took the first type of apples to the nobleman's house. Many people gathered around and robbed Nor-man of his apples. They ate their fill of apples, the lord eating the most of all. Soon everyone who had eaten the apples grew a nose so big that they could not move. Nor-man then went and got the other kind of apple, saying to all of them, "If you return the apple tree you stole, I will rid you of your big noses. Otherwise, you'll be dead in a minute." Everyone, including the lord, had no choice but to return the tree, which soon came back to life.

Nor-man went on to cure many more people with the magic apples. Since those days, people have eaten apples for strength and good health. Since ancient times, apple trees have spread around the world and greatly benefit humanity.

魔术

as told by
Du Jianhao

The Seven-Colored Flower

I live in Dalian, which is on the southern tip of Liaoning Province, on the Bo Hai Sea. There are many folktales from Dalian. One summer day I went to the shore to swim. As I sat on the beach, I got to know an old woman, who told me this beautiful and interesting folktale.

*L*ong, long ago, there was a pretty little girl who lived beside the sea. She was bright and lovely. There were three people in her family, her mother, her father, and her. Her parents loved her very much, and she loved them too. They lived a happy life in a little house by the sea.

Every evening the girl sat by the shore and looked at the wide sea. She often thought about the things on the other side of the sea and wondered what happened there. She longed to go there very much.

One night she had a beautiful dream. She saw a big, magnificent ship coming from the other side of the sea, stopping near her house. She was interested in the ship, so she boarded it and hid herself in a corner. The ship set out and, after six days, arrived at the shore. People began to take things out of the ship and found the girl, whom they took to see the king at his palace. At the palace, the girl saw an old man in golden clothing who turned out to be the king. This king had no daughter, so when he saw the little girl and found her to be lovely, he wished her to stay with him in his palace. The king asked her where she was from, and she replied, telling him all about her home and her family. She agreed to stay on and live as his daughter.

At first the girl lived happily in the palace, but after a month she thought about her parents and began to cry. The king asked her what was wrong, so she told him that she missed her family and wished to go back home. This made the king very sad, for he knew that he would never see the lovely little girl again. At last he agreed. Before she left, however, he wished to give her a present, so he took her to his treasure room and told her to choose something that she found beautiful. As she gazed into the room, she found it full of fabulous treasures. Suddenly her eyes fell upon a dazzling seven-colored flower made of jewels. She liked it very much so she chose it, and the king told her that the flower would allow her to make seven wishes come true. She thanked the king and went off to sleep for the night.

When the girl awoke in her own bed, she found the seven-colored flower lying by her side. She recalled her strange and beautiful dream as she lay there. When she finally got up, she accidentally knocked a vase off the table that belonged to her mother, a vase her mother treasured. The girl was frightened, but then she remembered the flower and the king's promise. She picked one petal of the flower and said, "Make my mother's vase as good as new." No sooner had she said this than the vase appeared in perfect condition on the table. The girl was happy and thanked the king in her mind.

The next day the girl was playing with a companion who had a toy, while she had none. This made her angry, so she picked another petal of the flower and said, "I want to have many toys." Immediately a pile of toys appeared. The pile of toys got bigger and bigger without stopping. The girl quickly picked another petal and said, "Please, flower, take these toys back," and the toys promptly disappeared. Her companion was dumbfounded.

After a year, the girl had only one petal of the seven-colored flower left. One day she saw an unfortunate boy who had no legs. The girl asked him what had happened, and he replied that when he was a child, an accident took away his legs. From that day on, he told the girl, he never played with other children or even by himself, but he dreamed of walking and playing like a normal boy. The girl was so moved that she took off the last petal of her flower and said, "Oh, seven-colored flower, please give this poor boy his legs back."

Suddenly the boy found that he had two perfectly fine legs. He stood up to walk and even run, and the two played together joyfully.

Harp Hole

as told by
Zhou Jing

When referring to my hometown, Dalian, people always say that it is a beautiful city, surrounded by sea and mountains. My hometown is a good place, where the air is fresh and the streets are clean. On the other hand, the prices are too high in Dalian, though I hope this problem will be solved soon. There is a story about a place in Dalian called Harp Hole that I once heard from my grandmother.

*I*t is said that long, long ago, Dalian was short of water. The fields were dry and the farmers had poor harvests. Year after year, the people who lived there were sick and hungry.

One day a beautiful girl in white with a black harp came to the area. She sat near a hole on the eastern side of a hill and started to play the harp. The sound of the harp was wonderful, like music from heaven. While people were intoxicated with the heavenly music, a miracle happened. As the girl played, spring water poured from the hole on the hill near where she sat. The water irrigated the farmers' fields, so crops could grow again and many people were saved. Surprised, the people crowded around the girl, who told them that the harp could bring them happiness and luck. They thanked her for what she had done and called her the harp girl.

Soon the harp girl had to leave. When the day came for her to go, the people were sad. They urged her to stay, but it was to no avail. Before the girl went away, she told the people that she had left the harp to them, placing it in the hole in the hill to the east of the village, where no one could find it. The people thanked her again, and she suddenly disappeared. The people realized that she was no ordinary girl, but a fairy maiden come to earth.

When the people went near the hole, they could hear the wonderful sound of the harp coming from it. Spring water flowed continuously into the fields and into the valley from the hole, and fresh, clear water was abundant.

Since that time, the area has never been short of water, and there has always been a good harvest. The people led happy lives from then on.

魔术

A Princess's Healing

as told by
Siu Wenli

I am from Shenyang, which is not only the capital of Liaoning Province, but also a center of heavy industry in northern China. With the development of the economy, many new buildings have appeared. Every night the darkness is dotted wonderfully with colorful lights from these many tall buildings. I like strolling along the street at night during the summer to appreciate these lights.

I once heard a folktale from a friend about an honest young man and a princess who was healed in an unusual way. I would like to tell you this story.

*M*any years ago, there was a flourishing kingdom in ancient China. Yet the king of this kingdom was not happy at all. He had a young daughter whom he loved deeply. Unfortunately, at the age of sixteen she had been stricken with a strange disease that left her blind. The king had ordered all of the famous doctors of the land to cure his daughter, but to no avail. They tried all kinds of remedies, but nothing seemed to work.

The old king still did not want to give up, so he sent out a proclamation to all parts of the kingdom. He promised to reward anyone who could restore his daughter's sight, adding that if this person were a young man, he would be permitted to marry her. As soon as the announcement was made, many people arrived at the palace claiming to be able to bring back the girl's sight, but none were successful.

At this time, there stood a lonely hut deep in the forest, where an old couple lived. This couple had had a hard life on account of their sons, two of whom caused them much grief. While the two elder brothers were very cunning, frequently telling the old couple lies, the youngest was honest and kind. Still, for some reason, the old couple did not like their youngest son.

This couple had a little knowledge of medicine, so when they heard the king's proclamation, they thought that fresh peaches might restore the princess's sight. The fresh peaches that the couple planned to have brought to the princess grew in the forest and thus were unavailable in town. The couple assigned the two eldest sons the task of carrying several sacks of peaches to the princess. As they walked to town, the two young men met a very old man dressed in rags, who asked them where they were from and what was on their backs.

Fearing that he would try to beg from them, they refused to answer his questions, saying impudently that they were cutting sticks and that branches were inside their sacks. Then they hurried on their way. At last they reached the king with the message that they had brought fresh peaches, which could help the princess see again. Full of hope, the king said to the two young men, "Let us see what is in your sacks.

To everyone's surprise, there were no fresh peaches at all, only branches and twigs. The king was furious, for obviously these two arrogant young men had played a trick on him. Puzzled, they were threatened with serious punishment and sent home in disgrace.

Not wanting to give up their chance of a reward, the old couple ordered their youngest son to try. Just as his brothers had done, he set out with a sack of peaches. He, too, met the old man dressed in rags. The young man pitied the poor old man, asking him whether there was anything he could do for him and giving him many peaches. When the old man asked him what he was doing in the forest alone, the young man explained that he was on a journey to try to help the king's daughter get her sight back. The old man said, "Luck is with you, my son. If you are ever in trouble, call me three times and I will help you."

Somewhat surprised by what the old man had said, the boy continued on his way. Finally he reached the palace, where the princess recovered her sight after eating some of the fresh peaches.

With the healing of the princess, some trouble came to the boy. Even though the princess had her sight back, the king did not want her to marry the young man because he was merely a poor villager. The king thought for some time, then decided to prove the boy unworthy, thus releasing himself from his promise. The king told the boy that before he married the princess, his honesty and steadfastness had to be tested. The king assigned him to care for some sheep, 100 in all. Then the king ordered his soldiers to steal one of the sheep, with the intention of blaming the boy for its loss.

When the boy came to the field the next day, he noticed one sheep missing. Fearing that he would be killed by the king, he suddenly remembered the old man he had met in the forest. No sooner had he repeated the man's name three times than the missing sheep reappeared in the field. The next day, when the king came and counted the sheep, to his surprise he found all 100 present. In the end, the king had to keep his promise and allow the young man to marry the princess.

魔术

as told by
Xue Mei

The Stone Horse

I come from Hubei Province, which lies in the middle of China. My hometown, Jingzhou, sits in the south of the Jianghan Plain, and the Yangtze River runs past it. Before Qin Shihuangdi united the different parts of China in 221 B.C., Jingzhou was part of the Chu Kingdom, a rich and creative culture. The famous poet Qu Yuan lived during the reign of the Chu. People still find many Chu cultural objects and ancient monuments in and around Jingzhou.

When I was a little girl, my mother often told me folktales. This is one of them. It is supposed to have happened in my hometown.

*L*ong, long ago, there was an old sculptor whose daughter was named Azhen. He and his daughter lived in a small village near Baiyun Mountain. He was well known for his skills and could carve all kinds of things out of stone, such as birds, horses, and fish.

At the foot of Baiyun Mountain, there lived a cruel officer of the county who wanted to have a stone statue for himself. Having heard of the old sculptor's skills, he sent for the old man and said, "I order you to carve a statue of me riding on a horse. You must finish it within a month. If you don't finish it by then, I will kill you."

The officer's threat was convincing, so the old sculptor had no choice but to comply with the order. After he arrived home, he found a piece of good stone and began to carve. Azhen, his daughter, helped him as his assistant. A few days later, the stone statue was finished. The horse statue was so beautiful that it looked real. But when the old sculptor and Azhen fit the statue of the officer on the horse's back, they were very unhappy.

The statue of the officer suddenly crashed to the ground and broke into pieces. The sculptor had smashed it. As he looked at the officer's statue on the horse, he became more and more angry. Finally he raised his hammer and destroyed the stone figure of the officer. Without the officer's statue, the horse looked more beautiful. The old sculptor and his daughter were very pleased with it.

A month went by. The cruel officer sent for the old man again and asked, "Have you finished my statue?"

"No, I haven't," replied the sculptor.

"No? How dare you disobey me! I'll have you killed!" The officer worked himself up into a terrific rage.

Hearing that the old sculptor was to be killed, the villagers themselves became angry and asked the officer to set the old man free. The officer realized that many people were against him, so he finally changed his order. He decided instead to send the old man away to do hard labor.

While he was away, the old man missed his daughter and the stone horse very much. Azhen stayed at home alone, and she, too, missed her father greatly. She often leaned against the horse, patted it, and told it her most heartfelt thoughts. She said, "Dear horse, my father is doing hard labor in a very distant place. How I wish I could see him!"

One day Azhen cried when she said those words to the stone horse. Her tears dropped into the eyes of the stone horse. The horse's eyes suddenly began to move. But even more shocking to Azhen was that the stone horse could speak. The horse said to her, "Don't cry, Azhen. I can help you find your father."

At first Azhen was afraid. She took several steps back, then looked at the horse carefully. He was staring back at her.

Azhen approached the horse. Hugging him, she said, "Dear horse, you're only made of stone. How can you help me?"

The horse replied, "First, you must help me become a real horse."

"But what can I do to help you become a real horse? Please tell me right away," Azhen said urgently.

"Listen to what I have to tell you," began the horse. "At the foot of Baiyun Mountain is a lake. Near the lake there are a lot of flowers. Among those flowers there are seven golden ones. Every day when the sun rises, these seven flowers open at almost the same time. Go there every morning and pick the flower that opens first and give it to me to eat. After eating the seven flowers, I will become a real horse."

Azhen did as he asked. After eating the seventh golden flower, the stone horse said to her, "Azhen, I will become a real horse. But first you must say to me, 'Stone horse, please become real and take me to look for my father.'"

Again Azhen did as she was asked, and before her eyes the stone statue turned into a snow-white horse. He flicked his tail and said, "Azhen, please get on my back. I will take you to look for your father after I drink water from the Gold and Silver River."

Azhen got on the horse, who immediately flew up into the sky. He flew so quickly that in only a few minutes they came to a mountain. The horse landed and told Azhen, "This is Treasure Mountain. While I drink the water of the Gold and Silver River, you may gather some treasure for yourself."

There was treasure all over the mountain, but Azhen said, "I do not want any treasure. I just want to see my father again."

When the horse had finished drinking, they flew once again. This time they went straight to the place where Azhen's father was forced to work.

When the old man saw Azhen, at first he thought that she was a dream. Azhen told her father what had happened, how the stone horse had come alive and brought her to him. The old sculptor was very pleased. He patted the horse's head and said, "Ah, my dear horse, you really are my good friend. Can you take us back to our home?"

"Of course," the horse answered. Azhen and her father climbed onto the horse's back, and they flew high into the sky.

Soon they came to Treasure Mountain again. The horse landed, telling them, "You can take some jewels if you like."

"But we can't take other people's treasures," Azhen and her father replied.

"No, this doesn't belong to anyone," the horse answered. "You both well deserve it. Take some."

Azhen and her father decided to take some riches and give them to the poor people of their village. After they had gathered some treasure, the horse carried them to town, where Azhen and her father gave away all of the jewels and still lived as they had before.

Several days later, the cruel officer heard that the old sculptor was back and that he and his daughter were giving away riches. Being greedy as well as cruel, the officer wanted the jewels for himself, so he sent several of his men to the sculptor's house to fetch the horse. The old man was again threatened with death if he failed to do as the officer said. Again the sculptor became very angry at the thought of giving his beloved horse away to such a wicked man.

The horse told the old man, "Don't be afraid. You may send me away with the officer. I can deal with him."

So the sculptor let the officer's men take the horse. Seeing the horse, the officer was so glad that he could hardly talk. He got on the horse with a very big bag. The horse flew up into the sky and disappeared into the distance. Neither the horse nor the cruel officer was ever seen again, and the old sculptor and his daughter lived happily ever after.

魔术

as told by
Zhao Dinghua

White Snake and Xuxian

My hometown is Dongyang in Zhejiang Province. Zhejiang is a beautiful province that is also the birthplace of many famous people, including Zhou Enlai. The capital of Zhejiang is Hangzhou, a very beautiful city famous for its West Lake. Thousands of people go to West Lake each year for vacation and relaxation.

The story of White Snake was told to me by my grandmother. The events in this story took place about a thousand years ago.

*L*ong, long ago, there was a boy named Xuxian. One day he saw a large group of people looking at something in the street. As the boy made his way over to the people, he noticed that someone was selling snakes. As the boy watched, the merchant took a little snake in his hand. It was a very strange little snake, all white. Though the man tried to sell the snake, no one wanted to buy it. The merchant wanted to go home but was unwilling to bring the strange white snake with him, so he decided to kill it and throw it away.

Xuxian felt sorry for the little snake, so he begged the merchant to give it to him. The man agreed and Xuxian ran to the field to set it free. Though the boy did not know it, the white snake was a ghost who could change herself into human form. She was grateful to him for saving her life. Some years later, she decided to reward him. But where was he and how could she find him? Soon she found out that the boy, now a young man, was living in Hangzhou. With her friend, Blue Snake, she went to the city to look for him.

Traveling in the form of two beautiful women, they searched Hangzhou for Xuxian, but did not see him anywhere. Eventually they came to Xihu Beach, where plays were being performed on a stage. White Snake was fascinated by the plays but, remembering why she had come, looked at everyone in the crowd hoping to see Xuxian. Suddenly Blue Snake pointed to a tree where a young man was perched reading a book. Using her magic, White Snake made it rain, forcing the young man to come down from the tree. The two women quickly went over to the man.

"Can I help you?" asked White Snake, with a slight smile and shining eyes.

The young man was nearly struck dumb by White Snake's beauty. When his eyes met hers, he blushed bright red and could only sputter, "I . . . I . . . Ahh . . . ." Then he was silent.

Blue Snake said, "Why not share this umbrella with us? It is raining hard."

At last Xuxian accepted. As they talked, White Snake found that the man was kind, handsome, and literate, and she fell in love with him. The young man found White Snake beautiful and kind, and he fell in love as well. White Snake followed him to his home and, realizing that she had found Xuxian, expressed her love for him. They married and lived together as if in a dream.

Their happiness was not to last. As a ghost, White Snake could not drink wine, for if she did she would change back into a snake. One day Xuxian insisted that she drink wine for a festival. Because she loved Xuxian so deeply, she took a sip. A terrible thing happened. Feeling dizzy, White Snake went to bed. After she had fallen asleep, she changed back into a snake. When Xuxian came into their bedroom, he was so shocked that he fainted and died.

When White Snake awoke, she found Xuxian dead. She was greatly grieved and regretted drinking the wine, feeling that she had caused her husband's death. She resolved to find the magic Linzhi plant that could bring him back to life. Because the plant only grew on far-away Quenlun Mountain and was guarded by the supernatural being Xiantong, she would have to steal it. White Snake flew to the mountain and was able to steal the magic plant. Just as she was about to escape, however, Xiantong attacked her. Fortunately, a powerful old magician, Nanji Xianwen, who knew White Snake, was able to order Xiantong to let her leave with the herb.

When Xuxian awoke, he told his wife what had happened to him. She replied that he had had a terrible nightmare and that she had never been a snake at all. Then she held Xuxian tightly to show him that she was a mortal being. Once again, as before, they lived the happy life of a couple in love.

Xuxian accepted White Snake's explanation of the strange events of that night and gave them no more thought, until one day when he went to Jishan Temple to make an offering. The priest, whose name was Faha, noticed something strange about Xuxian. Faha concluded that he was in some way connected with a ghost. At first Xuxian did not believe him, but when Faha told him more, he remembered the large snake he had seen in bed instead of his wife.

The more the priest told him, the more afraid Xuxian became. Faha told him suffering would come to him if he stayed with his wife and locked him up in the temple against his wishes. At home White Snake began to worry about Xuxian. After three days she went looking for him. At last she found out that he was locked in the temple. She asked the priest to free him, but he refused. Trying to force Faha to set her husband free, White Snake brought water from the sea to submerge the Jishan Temple. Faha, however, had powerful magic to resist the water. In the end, White Snake could do nothing but give up.

White Snake was dismayed as she left the temple, for she thought that she would never see her husband again. Just then she saw a man walking towards her. It was Xuxian, who had managed to escape from the temple after three days. Once again they lived together, as deeply in love as ever. This time Xuxian told White Snake that he would never leave her—snake, ghost, or woman. He would love her just the same.

Ghosts, Monsters, and Evil Spirits

Sea City

as told by
Chen Chang

I was born in Haicheng, Liaoning, in northeast China. Haicheng is a beautiful and prosperous city. Of all of the places I have been to, I think that my hometown is the most attractive one. There are mountains and water, as well as people I know. In China, Haicheng is quite famous for the Xiliu clothing market.

As a child, I loved sitting on my grandmother's knees, listening to her stories. She seemed to possess an endless store of them. One I remember well is the story of my hometown's name, Haicheng, which means "sea city." I would like to share it with you.

*L*ong, long ago, my hometown was a sea. All kinds of fish lived there, swimming happily. People in the nearby villages were fishermen. Life was frugal, but people were happy. Then one day in the spring, the blue sky was covered by threatening clouds, and the graceful sea began to seethe with terrible waves. All of the villagers hurried out to see what had happened. Suddenly a fearsome monster appeared on the surface of the water, with a mouth so gigantic it could swallow a boat. The monster announced to the townspeople that he would be there from then on, and he told the people, "You must follow my orders, or you will know the taste of my brutality." He laughed loudly and disappeared beneath the waves.

People were so scared that they did not know what to do. The monster became the master of the sea where the fishermen lived. No one dared to fish, because the monster would devour anyone he found on the water. Countless fish that could have been eaten by the hungry townsfolk instead ended up in the greedy monster's insatiable belly. The sea, once a source of joy, now brought only death.

There was a young man named Long in the village. He had always been smart and kind, helping people whenever he could. As a child, he had helped his father to chop down trees on the mountains and to fish in the sea. He was strong and brave. Seeing the misery the hateful creature caused his people, he began to think about how to kill it.

For many days people noticed Long leaving early and returning late without knowing what he was doing. Long was observing the monster secretly by the sea, searching for the monster's weakness. Eventually his efforts paid off. Long discovered that the monster was afraid of sunlight, preferring to stay at the bottom of the sea during the day. Long also discovered, to his surprise, that the monster liked alcohol and had looted a lot of wine from the village.

An idea occurred to him. One day before the sun made its appearance, Long, along with several youths from the village, brought dozens of jars of wine to the sea. They sat down in a circle, opened the lids, and drank and played. The desolate shore became lively. Soon, stirred from his sleep on the bottom of the ocean by the fragrance of the wine, the monster came to investigate the commotion on the shore. The young men paid no attention to the monster, but continued to drink and play. Angry at being ignored, the monster snatched a wine jar and drank it without stopping to take a breath.

"Give me another!" he shouted.

Long stood up among the young men and said, "How lonely to drink by yourself. Let's drink together. The one who drinks the most will rule our village. Nobody will disobey his orders."

Hearing this, the monster was very happy, for he felt sure that no one could outdrink him. Without a moment's hesitation he sat down and began to drink. He drank and drank and drank, until finally he could hold no more and fell down on the ground, motionless. The wine had been poisoned, but Long and his friends had taken an antidote so that they would not be affected. Though poisoned, the monster was not dead. Long and the other young men chained the creature tightly, putting lots of heavy wood on top of him so that he could not move. Finally they set the creature on fire. The monster cried out in pain and begged for his life, but to no avail.

By this time the people of the village had heard what had happened and came around to see the dying monster. They danced around the fire, jumping for joy and laughing. Slowly the animal died, but the fire continued to grow in size, threatening to swallow up the entire village. The people hurried to pour seawater to quench the fire. The fire was finally extinguished, but the sea had become dry land. Because people could no longer fish there, they planted crops, toiling day and night in their fields. Happily, the land was endless and fertile. In this place grew a thriving city. Its name is Haicheng—"sea city."

as told by
Zhao Ye

Bowl Mountain

I was born in Benxi, Liaoning. Benxi is in the southeastern part of Liaoning. It has a long history and is sometimes called Mountain City by the people there, because more than eighty percent of the area around the city is covered by mountains. Benxi is also called Coal and Iron City, because it produces large amounts of these two products. There are many rivers too, of which the longest is 464 kilometers. The mountains and rivers make for beautiful scenery.

Near Benxi there is a mountain shaped like a bowl. I once heard a story from my grandfather that explains why it looks like this. According to him, it happened a long, long time ago.

*O*nce upon a time, an old man and his three sons lived beside a river. They planted vegetables and raised pigs. The old man and his youngest son worked very hard, while the other two sons were somewhat lazy. Because the old man and the youngest son worked hard, they became wealthy and lived a happy life.

One day an ugly man came to their house, saying that he was the river spirit. He told them that they should give him half of their vegetables and all of the pigs they raised, or else suffering would be in store for them. The old man and his three sons were very surprised, for they had done nothing wrong.

"Why must we do this?" asked the old man.

"Don't ask why," responded the ugly man. "You live near the river, so you must do as I say." With these words he disappeared.

Several weeks later they gathered a big harvest. Of course, they did not give their vegetables and pigs to the spirit. One day the spirit came again, this time turning into a large demon with a dreadfully big mouth. He opened his enormous mouth and half of the vegetables and all of the pigs were drawn into it.

The demon sneered and said, "Next time you have a harvest, you must give me everything. You can call me at the river, and I'll come to take the food and pigs. If you don't, I'll destroy your house. Don't ask why, just do it!" Then he disappeared.

That year the family had little to eat. The old man was very angry and felt ill. "We must kill the spirit," the old man said.

"What can we do with him?" asked the oldest son. "He's a spirit and we are human beings."

The next son agreed with his elder brother and added, "I think we should leave this place, or the spirit will kill us."

But the old man refused to leave. "No," he said, "I was born here. "I won't leave this rich land for any other place." The old man continued, addressing his eldest son, "I hear there is a wise man in the East. Will you go there and ask him for a way to deal with this spirit?"

The eldest son agreed, so the next day he headed toward the East. Two days later he met an old man sitting under a tall tree. Beside him was a stone horse that had lost two teeth, and green grass was growing under its legs.

"Hello, old man. Do you know where there is a wise man in the East?"

"Yes," said the old man. "I am the wise man."

The eldest son got down on his knees and said, "I am sorry, Grandpa. Can you help me?"

The old man smiled and asked, "What can I do for you?"

"There is a spirit in the river in my hometown. He has treated us so badly that we can't live there anymore, but we don't want to leave. Can you tell me how to deal with this spirit?"

"Sure, but you must do some hard work," said the old man. "Look at this stone horse. It has lost two teeth. You must pull out two of your own teeth and fix them into the horse's mouth. Then the horse will turn into a real one. It will eat the grass under its legs, then take you to a place where you will find a magic bowl, and that bowl will kill the spirit. But before you go to that place, you must go through a mountain of fire and a sea. The air on the mountain will be very hot, but you must not cry out or you will be turned to cinders. When you cross the sea, the air will be very cold, but you must not cry out or you will be thrown into the sea." The old man finished with the words, "Well, this is a very difficult job, isn't it?"

The young man stood stupefied. He was too frightened to try the journey. When the old man saw this he said, "Don't worry. If you don't want to go, here is a box of gold. You can take it home and live on it."

The eldest son said good-bye to the old man, then began to think about all the things he could do with the gold instead of going home with it. Instead of returning to his father and brothers he went to the city, forgetting all about them.

One week later, when the eldest son failed to return, the old man sent his second son to look for the wise man. The same thing happened all over again. The second son met the wise man, was told of the dangers that awaited his trip to find the magic bowl, then decided to take the gold instead and go off to the city. Another week passed and neither son had returned home, so the youngest son said to the old man, "Father, I will go to the East to look for the wise man. You take care of yourself at home." The old man begged his young son to be careful, then let him go.

After two days, the boy met the wise old man sitting under the big tree. The old man told him the same thing he had told his brothers. Though the boy was frightened, he thought of his father and all of the suffering he had gone through. So he pulled out two of his own front teeth and fixed them into the mouth of the stone horse. No sooner had he done this than the stone horse turned into a real one and started eating the grass beneath its feet.

The young man mounted the horse, which carried him high into the air through a fiery mountain where there were raging flames. Though he felt like he was burning up, he did not cry out. Then they crossed a sea where the cold wind blew across his face like a sharp knife, cutting into his skin. He gritted his teeth but said nothing, remembering what the old man had told him. At last the boy came to the end of the journey and found the magic bowl, which he carried back home with him on the horse.

When the old man saw that his youngest son had returned home, he was very happy and felt much better. Gradually his health returned, and together he and his son worked hard tending their farm. Soon it was harvest time again, but they gave nothing to the river spirit.

One day the spirit reappeared, demanding vegetables and pigs as he had in the past. This time, instead of allowing him to devour their crops and animals, the youngest son threw the magic bowl at the spirit, trapping him under it. Soon the bowl began to grow bigger and bigger, eventually becoming a mountain.

As can be imagined, the youngest son and his father became wealthy again and lived happily together. One day two beggars passed through town, the two sons who had taken the gold and gone to the city. Their gold was used up and they had no way to make a living, so they had become beggars. When they saw their father and brother leading happy lives, they were so ashamed that they went away without even stopping.

So now you know why that mountain near Benxi is shaped like a bowl. Perhaps that spirit is still trapped under it and will come out some day. But what can we do? Perhaps it is best to forget about the nasty spirit who tortured the old man and his sons.

Sky Pool

as told by
Jing Yan

Shenyang lies in the center of Liaoning Province in northeastern China. It is the fourth-largest city in China. Shenyang has a long history. The Xinle ruins, which lie in northern Shenyang, prove that six thousand to seven thousand years ago, the people who lived here had a highly developed culture. Much later, the Qing capital was located in Shenyang.

In the northeastern part of China, many people are descended from the Manchus, the founders of the Qing Dynasty. There is a folktale popular among the Manchus about how a place called Sky Pool appeared. The story I would like to tell comes from my grandmother, who is of Manchu ancestry.

*L*ong, long ago, in the area that is now Jilin Province, there was a demon who liked swallowing fire. First he swallowed fire from the sky and the earth became dark. Then he swallowed fire from the ground and the world became cold. Finally he swallowed the fire used to cook, and human beings had nothing to eat. Because the people knew that the only thing the demon feared was ice, they gathered to drive the demon away using this element. At last the demon hid in a hole deep in the ground, which the people filled with stones and soil.

People sang and danced, believing that they had conquered the evil demon, but unfortunately it did not die. It swallowed fire from under the ground and became even more powerful. Suddenly, on July 15, a great fire erupted from under the earth that lasted for eighty-one days and destroyed many houses and trees. From then on, year after year, on July 15 fire would spurt from the earth and cause destruction for eighty-one days. During these difficult times people had no houses to live in and no food to eat, all of the flowers died, and the birds no longer sang. What could people do?

Now there happened to be a girl named Mukulun who saw the people enduring cold and hunger and felt very sorry for them. One day she noticed a swan flying overhead, so she asked it if she could borrow its wings to look for a god to help them. The swan was moved by her bravery and lent her his wings.

With the swan's wings, Mukulun found the wind god, who said he would help the poor human beings. When July 15 came and fire erupted from under the earth, the wind god blew up a terrible windstorm but this only strengthened the fire. So the wind god told the girl to go ask the god of rain to help her.

Mukulun once again flew into the air in search of a god. She flew to the sea to beg the rain god for help, and the rain god nodded. The heavy rain had no effect on the fire, so the rain god told the girl to call on the god of snow for help. Mukulun flew to the mountains to ask the snow god for help, but not even snow could put out the great fire.

Mukulun thought and thought. Was there no way to save her people? At last she decided to see if the god of the sky could help her, so she flew and flew until she met the sky god, who already knew of her plight.

The sky god told her, "You can save the human race. But are you willing to sacrifice everything for this task?"

Mukulun answered firmly that she would do anything for her people.

The sky god smiled and gave her a piece of ice, saying, "When the demon sprays fire onto the earth, you must fly directly into his mouth with this ice. It will put out his fire and make him harmless."

Mukulun went immediately to where the demon was raging fire. She flew into his mouth with the ice; though the fire burned her hair and smoke blinded her eyes, she did not turn back. Finally the fire went out and the demon died. Soon the grass and trees turned green, the flowers bloomed, and the birds started singing again. People began to sow seeds and build houses. The hole where the demon is buried, it is said, turned into a lake, which was named Sky Pool in memory of Mukulun.

It is also said that Mukulun did not die, but flew up into the heavens to thank the sky god. Because the god's wife liked her very much, Mukulun was allowed to stay with the god's six daughters, and together they came to be known as the "seven celestials." Mukulun often returns to Sky Pool to bathe with the god's daughters. Someday, if you are lucky, you may see them there.

Village Ghost

as told by
Tian Yang

I was born in Benxi, Liaoning. Liaoning Province has a number of important cities, including Shenyang, the capital of the province. Shenyang is the fourth largest city in China, as well as an economic center for the three northeast provinces.

When I was young, I stayed at my mother's aunt's home. My uncles and aunts were very kind to me. Every night before I slept, they told me a story. Some of these were mystical and others were horrible. I was timid, so I often had to hold on to an adult while I listened. Among those stories one deeply impressed me. Even now when I tell it, my hair stands on end. Here is the story.

A long time ago, there was a family in which the parents had many children, four sons and three daughters. The children were very naive, though smart and active, and the parents were brave, industrious, and hard-working. By day the parents worked in the field while the children played around them. At night the parents told stories until the children fell asleep. They were all quite happy.

One day the parents had to leave home for several weeks. The mother and father urged their children again and again to take care of themselves, especially at night, not to play outside after dark, and to go to sleep early. The children asked their parents to come back as soon as possible.

Now it happened that there was a ghost in the neighborhood who particularly liked to suck the blood of children. The ghost had slaughtered many children, and the villagers hated him to the very marrow of their bones.

The night the parents left, the ghost came to the house, but the door was locked. He knocked on the door, and, thinking their parents had returned, the youngest child went to open the door. When the door opened, the ghost grabbed the child and sucked all the blood from its body. When he had finished he threw the body into a nearby well. From then on, every night the ghost knocked on the door, killing one child, sucking its blood dry. Each time the children thought their parents had returned home. In this way all seven children were killed.

When the parents returned they were very grieved and furious, so they made up their minds to get rid of the ghost. They dug a snare in the front of the house with the help of the other villagers. Then they pretended that they had other children playing in the yard and that they had to leave as before.

When it was dark the ghost appeared again and fell unsuspecting into the snare. The villagers captured the ghost, which turned out to be a fox. The villagers put some of the fox's blood into the bodies of the children, who then revived, and they were all very happy once again.

A Family and a Ghost

as told by
Yao Li

I come from Shenyang in Liaoning Province. I like Shenyang very much because I grew up there. Shenyang has a number of folktales. The one I will tell is a ghost story from my grandfather. When he lived with us he often told stories, the most interesting of which is the following. Now let me tell it to you.

A long, long time ago, there were some people and some ghosts who lived in mountainous regions not far from the cities. Sometimes ghosts killed people who lived near them, so people stayed alert all the time.

One day a family—a couple and their three daughters—received a letter from their maternal grandmother saying that she was ill. Because the father worked far from home in the city and the two eldest daughters, aged twelve and sixteen, were old enough to stay by themselves, the mother decided to take her youngest daughter, who was eight, with her to the grandmother's home. Before she left, the mother told her two daughters that she would be away from home for a week and warned them to beware of ghosts.

"Be sure to keep the door closed," the mother warned. "If anyone knocks, you must not answer." Then the mother left with her youngest daughter.

Soon after the mother left, the daughters were looking forward to her return. On the third evening, when someone knocked at the door, the eldest asked, "Who's there?"

"Me! It's me. Your mother."

The two girls were very surprised, but they did not forget their mother's words. The eldest girl said, "You told us you would be back in a week. Why are you back so early?"

"Your grandmother is much better now and I have been worried about you, so I came back a bit early," came the answer. When the two girls opened the door to let their mother come in, they noticed that she was alone.

"Where is our little sister?" asked the eldest.

"She stayed at your grandmother's," came the reply. "Because she rarely goes there, your grandmother let her stay longer." The two girls believed her and let her in.

Soon it was time for bed. As they were getting ready to sleep, the eldest girl sensed there was something strange about their mother that she could not quite grasp. When she spied a tail underneath her mother's nightdress, however, she knew that whoever or whatever had come into their house was not their real mother.

Afraid that it was a ghost who would try to kill her and her little sister, she made a plan to get some help from their neighbors. In the middle of the night she said that she had to go to the bathroom, then slipped out quickly and asked the neighbors to surround their home and catch the ghost. Though the two girls were saved with their neighbors' help, to their dismay they discovered that their mother and sister had been killed on their way to their grandmother's. The ghost, knowing that the two remaining sisters were alone, had come disguised as their mother.

As she looked at the ghost, the eldest girl cried, "You killed my youngest sister and my mother. You wanted to kill me and my sister, too. But you won't! Never!"

The people captured and killed the ghost, making the village safer than before. Though they celebrated their victory, they were saddened that the mother and youngest sister had been killed. Because of the bravery of the eldest girl, she and her sister, as well as many other villagers, were saved. For this the people were grateful.

Sleeping Cow Mountain

as told by

Hua Li

I come from Nanyang, Henan. Nanyang is a small city that lies in the south of Henan Province. Mountains surround the city. It is very hot in the summer and very cold in the winter. Nanyang's mountains are the source of much jade, which is clear and beautiful. Every year a lot of jade is sold to other parts of China. People love the rings and statues made from it. Near Nanyang there is a mountain that is not very high but extends for a long way. It looks like a great cow sleeping, and, yes, it is called Sleeping Cow Mountain. This name comes from a very moving story that my grandmother told me.

*I*n ancient times Nanyang did not have this mountain, only broad, regular fields. The people who lived in this place were very happy. One hot summer day, things began to change. The wind began to blow and snow began to fall. A huge fireball blazed through the sky and dropped to the ground, destroying the golden wheat and green rice of the fields. The fire suddenly disappeared, but a small lake remained. The Highest God had driven a guard out of heaven for stealing, hurling him to earth as a great venomous snake to live in this lake. The snake wasted no time in terrorizing the people. It often flew out of the water, spraying poisonous liquid on the people and their crops.

Near the lake there lived a young man named Chun Sheng, whose parents had been killed by the snake. He hated the creature and was anxious to destroy it, so he went to a famous blacksmith who gave him a rare and powerful sword. Thinking that he might kill the snake with this weapon, he dared the snake to appear and fight. Enraged at Chun Sheng's daring, the snake flew at him and they began to fight. They fought for seven days and nights. Finally the snake was wounded and retreated back into the water, but Chun Sheng had been poisoned. He was dying and lost consciousness.

When he awoke, Chun Sheng found himself in his room. A beautiful girl stood beside him, smiling.

"Who are you?" Chun Sheng asked.

"I am a stranger here. I came to look for two relatives, but they both died. I found you near the lake."

Thanking her, he told the girl the story of how he had fought the snake. She was moved by his story, telling him, "I have no parents or home. Will you let me stay with you?" Chun Sheng liked the girl, so they married.

After one year, the couple had a boy. The boy grew up quickly. After some years he became taller than his father and as strong as a cow, so his father called him Black Cow. Chun Sheng never forgot that he had not killed the snake, but now he was old and weak. He could only let his son finish the task. Black Cow was a kind young man, and when he saw his people's suffering and poverty because of the snake, he was as determined to kill it as his father had been.

One day, while he was practicing with his father's sword in the forest, an old man with white hair appeared before him. The old man smiled and said, "You want to destroy the snake and help the poor, I know. But the snake is fierce and poisonous. You will be defeated like your father."

"What can I do?" asked Black Cow.

The old man replied, "I have a suit of clothing for you to wear. Wearing these clothes, you will be in no danger. But you must take them off as soon as you kill the snake, or you will become a real cow."

"Thank you," said Black Cow, bowing to the old man.

The next day Black Cow got up early and put the clothes on. He told his parents not to worry, that he was sure to kill the snake. Then he left. He fought the creature day and night until both were exhausted. At last he seized the snake by the neck and prepared to kill it, but it pretended to weep and begged for its life, promising to do no more harm if its life were spared. The kind Black Cow hesitated, believing its words. Sensing the young man's indecision, the snake suddenly rushed to bite him. Black Cow realized that he had been deceived. He became very, very angry and cried out in a loud voice, "I will kill you!" and tried his best to fight against the snake.

During the struggle Black Cow managed to split the snake into several parts, and blood flowed into a nearby lake, turning it red. Though he had killed the snake, he was so weary that he forgot to take off the magic clothes the old man had given him. He lay on the ground and fell asleep, slowly turning into a mountain that encircled the village. In great sorrow and to remember Black Cow's bravery and kindness, the villagers called the mountain Sleeping Cow.

Moon's Shadow on the Water

as told by
Zhou Yang

I am from Changshu, Zhejiang. Of all of the places to see in Zhejiang Province, probably the most famous is the beautiful port city of Hangzhou. The scenic West Lake is in this city. There is a story about a stone in this lake, which I would now like to tell.

*I*n Hangzhou, there was once a famous and skilled craftsman named Lu Ban. He had a beautiful sister named Xiao Mei. The brother and sister did many good things for the common people, and for this they were greatly respected.

One day, as Lu Ban and his sister were out walking, Xiao Mei was seen by the monster who lived in the lake. Immediately he came out of the water and asked Xiao Mei to marry him. She refused, of course, so the monster became very angry. He told her that he could give her plenty of treasure, but still Xiao Mei refused, telling him that she would die before she married him.

Finally the monster shouted that if she did not marry him he would kill her. Xiao Mei was frightened, but the monster did not kill her. He wanted her to think about his offer instead, so he waited three days for her reply. On the first day, the water of the lake rose, covering some of the farmland nearby. On the second day when she still had not answered, the water rose still higher, covering half of Hangzhou. Finally, on the third day, the entire city was underwater. Many people were homeless and had climbed to the top of a nearby hill to save themselves. ·

Xiao Mei did not want the people to suffer any longer, so she and her brother discussed the matter. When they had finished talking, Xiao Mei cried to the monster, "Okay, I agree!" The water receded immediately, and the monster danced for joy.

Lu Ban said to him, "I have only one sister and I want her to marry with dignity, so I will fashion a suitable dowry for her."

The monster was very happy, agreeing without further thought, and asked Xiao Mei what she wanted her brother to make. Pointing to a boulder on the peak of a nearby mountain, she said, "I want Lu Ban to make that big stone on the hill into an urn for burning incense." Lu Ban gathered his tools and began to work, but progress went slowly, owing to the size of the huge rock and its position on top of the mountain. As Lu Ban's work continued, the monster became very impatient, pressing for its completion every day.

After some time it was finally finished, but the urn was far too heavy to move. The monster laughed at the people's feeble attempts to move the immense object. Then he took a deep breath and heaved the urn into the air, intending to catch it and carry it down to the lake. The urn, however, being even heavier than he had imagined, fell upside down on top of him, then rolled down to the lake with the monster inside. It came to rest upside down in the lake, trapping the monster, with one of the urn's legs showing above the water.

The place where the urn's foot sticks out of the water has become a place of interest at West Lake. It has a nice name, Moon's Shadow on the Water. At night, when the moon's reflection hovers over the water, it is said that you can hear the monster, still trapped under the urn, crying.

Python Mountain

as told by
Liu Ning

I come from a beautiful province, Guizhou. Guizhou lies in the southeastern part of China, close to Sichuan and Yunnan. Guizhou has a good climate, not too hot in the summer and not too cold in the winter.

My hometown, Duyun, lies in the south of Guizhou. It is a small city, and it takes only two hours to walk from one end of it to the other. The Sword River, over which there are more than twenty bridges, circles the city and gives Duyun its other name, Bridge City. Around the city stand many mountains, the highest of which is called Python Mountain. My story comes from my grandmother and is about this mountain, the Sword River, and its bridges.

*L*ong, long ago, Duyun was only a small village. The villagers led a quiet, happy life hunting and planting, until one day a strange and horrible thing happened. While the people were busy going about their daily business, the wind suddenly started to blow so hard that they all had to shut their eyes. Clouds covered the sky. All of the men were in the forest hunting, but when they saw the dark clouds and felt the strong wind, they hurried back to town. There they found all of the animals gone, the women frightened, and the children in tears.

As the women and children told it, a python ghost had come and informed the villagers that they should present him a cow, a goat, and a pig every month, or else he would destroy the village. On hearing this, the men were very angry, but no one dared to volunteer to kill the monster until a young man named Aming stepped out of the crowd. Aming was the strongest, bravest, and brightest man in the village. Whenever the men of the village went hunting, Aming always captured or killed the most game. Aming made up his mind then and there to get rid of the python ghost, even if doing so cost him his life.

Before setting out, Aming made careful preparations. First he went to the best blacksmiths, asking them to make the sharpest sword for him. Then he chose the best bow and gathered the men to grind the hardest stones into arrows. All this cost him forty-nine days; then he left amid wishes for his success from his fellow villagers.

Aming set out for the mountain where the python ghost was believed to live. The mountain had a dark cloud hovering over it and was farther away than it seemed. He had to climb over three hills and cross five forests before he got to the cave where the ghost lived. When Aming finally arrived at the cave, he shouted, "Deadly ghost, come out and meet your death!"

Before long the evil ghost appeared. He was terribly angry and said, "How dare you defy me! I'll eat you alive!" Then he attacked Aming, who defended himself with his sword.

One day passed in combat and neither had killed the other. The second day passed with the same result. On the third day, Aming thought of a way to defeat the ghost. He pretended to be scared and fled, but soon found a good hiding place. He took his bow and a stone arrow, aimed carefully, and let the arrow fly. Unfortunately, the shot hit the ghost's leg, which only made him madder. He changed into a very, very large python, sliding toward Aming with an open mouth.

Aming calmly shot at the python, but all of his arrows merely bounced off the creature's thick skin. Soon the python reached Aming, coiled around him, and began to crush him.

Even while this was happening, Aming remained calm. He lifted his heavy bow and began to beat the python across the head and eyes. On the tenth stroke, the creature died. Aming used his remaining strength to hurl the snake off of himself, then he too collapsed and died.

Aming had thrown the snake nearly a quarter of a mile, and where it fell it turned into a mountain. At the same time, Aming's sword changed into a river and his arrows into bridges over the river. From then on, the people of Duyun called the mountain Python Mountain, and the river Sword River. The villagers built a tower to remember their hero, which they named after him.

The Story of Huang Yang Boundary

as told by
Wang Boran

My hometown is in Lichuan County in Jiangxi Province. Jiangxi lies in the southern part of China, a region with green hills and clear waters, full of beautiful scenery. Jiangxi is also the home of rice and fish, with a large freshwater lake, called Poyang Lake. People in the area have lived and worked in peace and contentment for many years. Some people farm on both sides of Poyang Lake, while others make their living by fishing on the lake. Because of the tranquil weather on the lake and fair weather in the fields, it would seem that there is no trouble in this region. However, I will tell you a story that may affect you quite a bit. This story comes from a friend of mine, who is also from Jiangxi.

*O*ne day a terrible monster appeared in Poyang Lake. It was said that the monster had three heads and six arms, with a ten-meter-long body. When he was happy, he would rest quietly; otherwise, he would incite trouble and cause confusion in the lake. Then he would soar into the air, creating a tremendous wind accompanied by thunder and lightning. Strong gusts would begin to blow and dark clouds would form; heaven turned upside down when the monster was angry. As a result, crops were flooded, boats were overturned, and many people died. However, the people of the town had no idea how to deal with this powerful and violent creature.

At that time, there was a little boy named Huang Yang. His parents had both been killed by the monster. Little Huang Yang promised with tears in his eyes and a hoarse voice that he would rid the lake of the monster with his own two hands. But he was young and the monster was powerful, so it was impossible for him to kill the monster using only his own strength. Little Huang racked his brain for days trying to figure out how to kill the creature. He even stopped caring about food.

At last Little Huang made up his mind to learn Wu Shu,* although many people tried to persuade him not to go through with this. Little Huang cried, "I must avenge the deaths of my parents and all the others. I would rather die if you won't let me go!"

The entire town stood without saying a word. The townspeople did not have the heart to see him suffer from not being able to do anything, so they finally agreed to let him go even though he was just a little boy. Besides, almost no young men were left, for they all had been drowned or eaten by the monster. The miserable townspeople had no choice but to see Little Huang off, which they did with tears in their eyes. They prayed silently for him as he left.

Little Huang set out on his trip. He climbed ninety-nine mountains, waded across ninety-nine rivers, and wore out ninety-nine pairs of shoes. When he was hungry he stopped and ate a bit of dry food, and when he felt sleepy, he napped on the bare ground. At last Little Huang arrived at Lu Hill, where an old magician lived whom he had heard about from his parents. The magician was moved deeply by Little Huang's sincerity, so he agreed to take him on as his apprentice.

---

* *Wu Shu is the general term for various kinds of Chinese boxing and fencing.*

Nine years passed in the twinkling of an eye. Huang Yang grew up bit by bit and became a strong young man with great skills in Wu Shu. Finally he thought that it was high time for him to return to his hometown. Before he left, however, the old magician gave him a sharp, double-edged sword and a magic horse. The sword could cut iron or steel like mud, and the horse could run 1800 miles a day and also had wings to fly. Huang Yang cried when he parted with his teacher, then he hurried to his hometown.

Just before he entered the town, the monster, who had terrorized the townspeople all those years, flew overhead, laughing heartily at the frightened people on the ground. A dark sky covered the sullen earth, and it seemed as though disaster would soon strike again. Anger grew in Huang's heart. Deciding that it was high time the killer of his parents and friends were destroyed, Huang flew into the air on his magic horse, stabbing the monster with his sword. The two fought terribly in the sky, the monster lunging at Huang with his sharp claws.

One day passed, then two, and they were still fighting. Thunder boomed and lightning flashed, while rain poured down. By this time both Huang and the monster were injured, and Huang's strength was nearly exhausted. Huang knew that he was close to death, but he wanted to rid humankind of such a dangerous menace, no matter what the cost to him. With all of the strength he could muster and a loud scream, he lunged forward, driving his sword straight through the belly of the monster and out of its back. He had killed the monster of Poyang Lake.

Huang Yang stood quietly with the sword in his hand. Soon a mysterious change began to take place, for he was gradually transformed into a great stone. This stone is now called Huang Yang Boundary in his honor. Because of this stone, people will not forget the beautiful and moving story of this brave young man who devoted his life to making Poyang Lake safe.

Madame Qin

as told by
Yang Jianyou

*I*come from Tangshan, Hebei. Tangshan lies northeast of Beijing. It is the biggest industrial city in Hebei Province and abounds in coal and steel. A large power station in Tangshan supplies electricity to north China.

On the evening of July 28, 1976, a great earthquake turned Tangshan into a large ruin. About 240,000 people were killed, and thousands of children became orphans. The city has since been rebuilt and is now a thriving commercial and industrial center.

When I was a child, my mother often told me interesting and strange stories. The one that impressed me the most was about an elderly woman who died and came back to life again.

*M*adame Qin was a woman about eighty years old who was in very good health. One day, however, she became very ill and said that she would soon die. She asked her family to gather around her, for she wished to see them one last time. Her little granddaughter, however, lived far away, and it would take five days for her to arrive. No one thought that the woman could wait until her granddaughter's arrival, but she did not die until the girl arrived. After saying a few words to the girl, Madame Qin died. The family was very sad, and the little granddaughter cried herself sick, for she loved her grandmother very much.

Finally the family made preparations for the funeral. However, a strange thing happened on the second day of the ceremonies. Three days after the woman had died, a man suddenly heard a voice from her coffin. It sounded like the cry of a woman, and the man was so afraid that he ran from the coffin. No one dared to go near the coffin except the granddaughter, who said that it must be her grandmother, who was living again. No one believed her, so she went to the coffin and opened it herself. When she did, she saw her grandmother sitting in the coffin. Madame Qin asked why she had been shut up in such a dark box. The girl was so happy that she did not say a word; she just hugged the old woman with tears in her eyes. When everyone came to the room, they were amazed and could not believe what they saw.

The old woman told her family that she had dreamed a very strange dream. She dreamed that she was dead and had come to the land of ghosts. It was a beautiful place, she said. There were flowers all around and many houses in this place. The ghosts lived happily, just as people in this world do. She said that she talked with them, and they told her that they live there very happily and have families. Men have wives and women have husbands. They also have children, but their children were not born to them in our way. They said that when a person in the human world died, she would turn into a baby and come to the ghost world as the child of a couple. Also, when a person in the ghost world died, she would be born to a couple in the human world. They said that a ghost can remember her life in the human world, but a ghost who returns to the human world forgets everything that happened to her before she came to the land of the humans. They also said that they can come to the human world to see their relatives occasionally, but that humans never know about it.

After they told her all of these things, the ghosts took her to visit their king in his palace. The king asked her why she had come to the land of the ghosts. She was very surprised and answered that she had died. Then she asked why she had not turned into a child. The king answered that she had not died and that her time in the human world was not over yet. Then he sent her to a mountain valley and she was scared. Next thing she knew, she awoke and found herself in a dark coffin.

It is said that Madame Qin is still alive today, and that she is in even better health than before.

The Dead Man

as told by
Zhu Wei

I live in Anhui Province, one of the poorest provinces of China. Many people from Anhui want to move to other parts of China and abroad to make a better living. Tourists, however, come to Anhui to climb Huangshan, or Yellow Mountain, one of China's holy mountains. My hometown is in Suixi County, where there is nothing famous to speak of. Its people are simple and not unlike those from many other parts of China.

I would like to tell a strange story that is well known in my hometown.

*O*ne hot noon, a man arrived at his house and found his wife senseless, lying on the floor. He put his hand on her forehead, only to discover that she was cold and had probably been dead for some time. When the doctor arrived, he examined the woman, coming to the conclusion she had taken poison. The husband was puzzled. In deep sorrow, he had no choice but to bury his lovely wife. Still confused and grieving, the husband and his small son tried to resume their life as it had been before the woman died. Days passed, and before long two weeks had gone by.

One day, while he and his son were sleeping, the door suddenly opened by itself. The husband woke up immediately and, to his amazement, a woman in white entered. It was his wife.

Shocked, the husband cried, "Why did you leave us, our son and me?"

The woman replied, "Don't blame me. I did not leave willingly. I will tell you what happened." She sorrowfully told her husband all that had befallen her.

The day she died she had been lying on the sofa watching television when a strange man came in. She said he was handsome, but there was something horrible about him.

"Who are you? Why didn't you knock before you came in?" she asked, trembling, for she felt that something terrible was about to happen. The man did not answer, but came toward her and gave her a bottle of poison. She wanted to refuse, to call for help, but she could not; something kept her from screaming. She wanted to struggle, but she had no strength. She tried not to take the bottle, but her hand seemed to be someone else's. Her right hand grasped the poison and brought it to her mouth. She swallowed the poison, fell to the ground, and died, while the man left the room noiselessly and unseen by anyone.

The woman became a ghost. She followed the man through a wide plain, eventually reaching his room. The man then told her that he had mistakenly been taken to the spirit world by the king of the ghosts. He would have been alive, he told her, but the king had confused him with another man who had died a year before. Unable to bring him back to life, the king promised to let him take three wives from among the living. He already had two and she was the third, he told her.

In the ghost's home, the man's other ghost wives often beat the woman and forced her to do all of the cooking and washing. She could not bear it anymore. On a day when the man and his other two wives went to town, she insisted she did not want to go. She told her husband that though she had come to speak to him, she must return to the ghost world, for she had been told by the man that if she went back to her family, her son and husband would be in danger.

"Don't be afraid," her husband said angrily. "If they come, I'll protect you."

The woman sadly replied that he was powerless against a ghost and could not do anything. Then she left sadly.

After his wife had left, the husband thought to himself that if he, too, were a ghost, perhaps he could defeat the man who had killed his wife. He wrote out a note requesting that his brother bring up the son. The following day he hanged himself, for it is well known that the ghost of a man who has died that way is very powerful.

After his death, he left home and began to look for the man who had killed his wife. Whenever he met other ghosts, he would ask them if they had seen a man with three wives. They all replied that he must have been a ghost for a short time indeed, for there were many ghosts with two or more wives. The husband went around for some time looking for his wife but had no luck at all. One day he sat by the bank of a river to rest; suddenly he overheard someone say his wife's name. He could not hear clearly, so he walked closer. A man was threatening to beat his wife if she cried out. A fight ensued in which the husband struck the ghost. The ghost struck back, knocking the husband to the ground. The ghost walked away smiling.

Feeling that a great injustice had been done to him and his wife, the husband decided to go speak to the king of ghosts. Unfortunately, the king told him that he could do nothing.

"We are ghosts," the king explained. "This is the way things are here. I am sorry."

Enraged but powerless, the husband roamed the streets in silence.

History and Legend

历史

as told by
Zhu Ri

Fenghuang Mountain

I am from Fengcheng County in Liaoning Province. My hometown, Dandong, is a very beautiful town with two rivers running through it and many hills around it. A famous mountain, Fenghuang, sits near our town. It is grand and looks like a guard protecting us. It is a very interesting place, especially when you climb it. In recent years, many tourists have come to visit Fenghuang Mountain, but it is still a dangerous place and full of adventure.

Why do people call the mountain near our town Fenghuang?* I often asked my grandfather this question. He told me the story of how the mountain got this name during the Tang Dynasty. Here is the story.

*Fenghuang means "phoenix."

A Tang emperor once visited northern China and heard that there was a beautiful bird called *fenghuang*, which lived in a cave on the mountain. He wanted to see this bird, so he went to the cave with his courtiers. The bird was sleeping when he arrived, but the emperor was impatient and put a long pole into the cave to awaken the bird. The *fenghuang* was startled and flew away, to the dismay of the emperor, who ordered his servants to plant colorful parasols on the mountain in the hope of attracting the bird. The emperor also ordered that the mountain be called Fenghuang Mountain from then on. The bird never did come back, though to this day there are still many Chinese parasols on Fenghuang Mountain.

About a hundred years later, a famous, high-ranking military officer, Xue Li, came to the area to fight against a minority nationality. He was a very capable warrior, especially good with his bow and arrows. After arriving in our little town, he was attracted by the beautiful view and rested there, stopping on a small hill just opposite Fenghuang Mountain. Xue Li noticed that there was a cleft between two tips of the mountain. He told his soldiers that he could shoot an arrow between the two peaks. Nobody believed his words; the soldiers said it was too far and the peaks were too close together. Nevertheless, Xue Li stood up and raised his bow toward Fenghuang far in the distance. He let an arrow fly, and several minutes later a great sound was heard. Everyone present saw that a hole had appeared between the two tips of the mountain, and they all cheered. From that day on, the hill on which Xue Li stood has been called Faxiangling, which means "Sent the Arrow Hill." Even today, if you stand on Faxiangling, you can see the hole on Fenghuang Mountain created by Xue Li's arrow. The hole is a cave, big enough for a person to walk through to the other side of the mountain, as if it were a gate.

The Prince River

as told by
Zhang Wanguo

I come from Benxi in Liaoning Province. Liaoning is the center of heavy industry in China. It has a base of steel, iron, coal, machine, and chemical industries. With recent developments, Benxi and Liaoning have been growing rapidly and playing a very important role in China today.

In our city, the Prince River runs through the entire city. When I was a child, my grandmother told me a story about how the river got its name.

*L*ong, long ago, there was a king. He had a very good son, who was handsome and clever and did many things the common people could not do while he was growing up. It happened that his father was getting old. One day the king called his son to him and said, "My son, I am old. I want to give my power to you. Can you keep it wisely?"

"Certainly," answered the prince.

A few years later, the king died, leaving a very prosperous country to his son. The queen, a very affectionate woman, helped her son with the business of being a king. The young king, however, did not give all of his attention to the matters of the country. He overindulged in wine and women while his mother waited patiently for him to realize the error of his ways. But the young man did not care. So, shortly after his father's death, the young man impoverished his country. People became destitute and homeless, and officials did not work hard but wanted only to get more money from the people.

Eventually the neighboring nation noticed this and invaded, taking the young king prisoner. In the end, the king lost all the fruits of the lifelong work of his father. To make matters worse, he was banished to a distant place. His mother was very disappointed in him and saddened by all that had happened.

In exile, the young king was forced to work very hard for long hours, while soldiers in charge of him laughed and jeered. At first he was not used to such work, but before long he became accustomed to hard labor. While he worked he had lots of time to think about his past life as a prince. He also recalled the destruction of his nation. So that he would not forget his homeland, he rose very early every morning, kneeling in the direction of his country. He told himself, "I must work hard. When I take power again, I must regain everything I have lost."

One day he received a letter from his mother. In it she told him of her advancing years and how she wished to see him once more before she died. She also told him that she would wait for him on the tallest tower in the land, so that she would be able to see him coming. Tears sprang to his eyes when he read her letter. The young king did eventually make it back to his homeland, but the ending is not a happy one. As he was nearing his homeland, in sight of his mother, a great wind lifted him off his boat and flung him into the river, killing him. Grief-stricken, his mother threw herself off the tower and also died. Since then, our river has been called the Prince River.

历史

as told by
Sun Jing

Why Manchus Do Not Eat Dog

*I*come from Dandong, a very beautiful city in the eastern part of Liaoning Province, on the border of North Korea. There are many hills nearby, as well as the beautiful Yalu River. Dandong is near the sea, so every summer people go there to escape the heat. Nearby Fenghuang Mountain is very famous, and many people want to climb it.

There are many beautiful places in Liaoning, as well as stories about the hills, rivers, and heroes of my province. Among these stories, perhaps the most famous is about the leader of the Tartar tribes, the first Qing emperor, whose name was Nurhachi.[*] I heard this story from my father.

[*] Nurhachi (1559–1626) was the leader of various Tartar clans, whom he unified to fight the Ming Dynasty. Nurhachi founded the Qing (or Manchu) Dynasty, which ruled China for more than 250 years.

*I*t is said that when Nurhachi's mother gave birth to him, the clouds in the sky parted and thunder rang out. A dragon descended from the heavens, and a boy's cry was heard—Nurhachi was born.

When the boy grew up, he realized that the emperor of the Ming Dynasty treated his people very badly. Nurhachi swore that he would change these unfair things. At that time, however, the Tartars were not united and frequently fought one another for land and riches. Nurhachi realized that before he could fight the Ming, he must unite the Tartars.

When Nurhachi was still a young man, both his father and grandfather, leaders of several Tartar clans, were killed by another man, who took their place by making a pact with the Ming emperor. Eventually Nurhachi was able to take revenge on the killer, putting him to death.

In an effort to unify the fragmented clans, Nurhachi fought many battles with other Tartars. In one battle, Nurhachi was seriously wounded by an arrow. The enemy attempted to catch him and kill him, but his horse, realizing that Nurhachi was in danger, ran into some high grass where they could not be seen.

Having lost much blood, Nurhachi fainted, falling off his horse to the ground. The horse, not knowing what to do, walked slowly in circles around his master but could not rouse him. Finally the horse wandered off, leaving Nurhachi lying unconscious in the grass. Meanwhile, the enemy commander, suspecting that Nurhachi was hiding somewhere in the tall brush, ordered his men to set fire to the entire area. Falling in and out of consciousness, Nurhachi had no idea that he was in danger of being burned to death.

Just when all seemed lost, however, Nurhachi's black hunting dog appeared. Though he barked and barked in an effort to wake his master, Nurhachi was too badly injured to rise. As the fire was nearing, the dog bounded towards the river and returned dripping wet. This he continued to do time and time again, until the grass was so wet that it could not burn. When Nurhachi came to, he discovered that all of the grass near him was wet. He saw his exhausted dog lying on the ground and the burned grass nearby. Having given all of his strength to save his master, the dog then died. When Nurhachi realized what his dog had done for him, he cried.

Nurhachi remained hidden from the enemy, and soon his friends arrived with his horse and reinforcements. After Nurhachi recovered from his wounds, he fought with renewed strength against the rival

Tartar clans, soon becoming supreme leader of them all. Since the day their leader was saved by his faithful hound, Manchurian Tartars never again ate the meat of dogs.

历史

as told by
Yue Lihua

White Tower Park

I come from Liaoyang in Liaoning Province. The city is small, but very old. It lies in the eastern part of Liaoning Peninsula.

Liaoyang has two reservoirs and the Taizi* River, which runs through the city. In one folktale, a prince jumped into the river and killed himself a long time ago. A beautiful park named Taizi River Park was built a few years ago. There is another park named White Tower Park. The white tower in this park is at least eight hundred years old, and there are many folktales about the tower. This is a story my older brother told me when I was a child.

Taizi means "prince."

*L*ong, long ago, Liaoyang was the center of northeastern China. At that time the city was the capital of an ancient empire, and it was not named Liaoyang then. The king was a wise man and was kind to his people. He let all of his people have a chance to give him suggestions, and he gave a present to the person who gave him the best suggestion. Thus he became a successful king. He helped his people become rich and also made the city very beautiful. Later, he decided to build a tower so tall that everyone in the city could see it.

The king thought for a long time about what shape the tower would be, then finally decided that it would be white and have eight sides, one for each of the eight directions of the compass. Because most people in China were Buddhists at that time, the tower would have figures of the Buddha on each side. The king also decided that the tower would have thirteen stories. Having decided all of these things, he had artists draw sketches of the tower, then handed these over to his officers to arrange to have the tower built.

The officers surveyed the city for several days, then chose the place that best fit the tower. The work began. Thousands of people joined the work force, and many skilled workmen were invited from all over China. Because there were no mountains near the city, stone had to be carried from far away. Materials for bricks also had to be brought from afar, so it took a long time to gather all of the supplies for the tower. Meanwhile, more and more workmen joined in the construction. Finally, when all of the materials had been brought to the site, the tower began to rise with great speed.

After the tower was half built, however, a serious problem stopped the work. In those days, there was no machine strong enough to carry the heavy bricks and stones high enough for the work to continue. For some time the workers stood idle and the tower no longer grew.

When the king learned of this problem, he became angry and ordered his officers to find a solution as soon as possible. The officers became so worried that they lost a lot of weight in only a few days, but still they came up with nothing. In desperation the officers announced to the people of the empire that whoever could find a solution to the problem would receive a handsome reward. Though everyone in the empire thought about the problem for some time, no one could come up with a way to raise heavy stones and bricks to the top of the tower. There were not even any suggestions.

One day an old man came to the city. He wore white clothes and had a very, very long beard and white hair. He was kindly and reserved, as though one of the gods had come to earth. Every day the old man quietly went about town, minding his own business. After some days he began to draw people's attention, and the officers asked him to come and see them at once. They treated the old man well, taking him to see the half-built tower and asking him if he could propose any solution to their problem.

The old man gazed at the tower for a while, then said, "I am only an old man. I am so old that my body is already half buried in the earth. You must use your brains to think." Then he went away and disappeared.

The officers looked at one another; they did not understand what the old man had meant, but guessed that there must be a solution in his words. All of the people in the empire thought about what the old man had said, but no one knew what it meant. The officers reported the man's words to the king, who thought about them for three days and nights. Finally he understood. The old man's solution was to bury half of the tower in earth, then carry the materials up to the top. The king announced the solution to his officers, and immediately work on the tower resumed.

The workmen carried a lot of dirt to the tower and piled it up until they could easily carry the heavy materials to the top. Once again the tower grew quickly and was soon finished. When the tower was completed, the workers removed the earth. The tower appeared exactly as the king had designed, and before long it became famous. Since then many people have come to Liaoyang to visit this ancient white tower.

历
史

as told by
Xia Bo

Wang'Er Hill

I am from Dalian, which lies in the eastern part of Liaoning Province, on the sea. Dalian has many pretty views, in addition to good weather. People from all over the country go there for holidays and for business meetings.

I once heard this story from a stranger on the train between Shenyang and Dalian about a place called Wang'Er Hill. If you take this train, about halfway between the two cities you will see Wang'Er Hill. *Wang'Er* means "waiting for the date of the son's return." The hill is not very big, but on top of it sits a large stone that looks like an old woman standing there waiting for her son. Her expression is sad and helpless, but still there is a spark of hope in her eyes.

*L*ong, long ago, where the hill now stands, there was not land but the sea. There was a small village near the sea. The villagers lived simply, working from sunrise until sunset. They planted vegetables, raised animals, and went out to fish. Still they were very poor, for all of these things were taken by their cruel landlord.

The short, fat landlord was very wealthy, but he was never satisfied with what he had. Even in his dreams he imagined great treasures of gold and silver falling from the sky, but when he awoke and found that this was only a dream, he became angry. He continually thought up ways to get more money out of the villagers. He obliged them to work for him, saying that their grandfathers or great-grandfathers had not paid off their debts to his grandfather. He took everything the villagers raised, planted, or fished without any thought to their survival. To make matters worse, the villagers dared not rebel for fear of the landlord's hatchet men. Anyone who showed the slightest resistance to the will of the landlord was threatened with death.

A young villager named Ahai was extremely resentful of the landlord, whose cruel ways had made his mother's life difficult indeed. His father had died when Ahai was just six, and he lived with his mother, who was now old and weak. Since her husband had died, she had had little happiness. She brought up her little son by herself, enduring much misery for the sake of her child. To pay the high taxes the landlord demanded, she worked harder and harder, swallowing insult after insult for ten years. By the time Ahai grew up, he was strong, brave, and clever. When he was only nine, he could already operate the rudder on a fishing boat and went to sea to fish.

Ahai was not afraid of the landlord. He secretly made plans against him, openly refusing to work for him or to pay taxes. He often called upon the villagers to revolt. Soon the landlord became wary of Ahai and decided to find a way to get rid of him. One day when Ahai was away from home, the landlord led a group of his men to Ahai's cottage. When the old woman came out and saw them, she knew that something bad would happen. The landlord instructed his men to catch the old woman, and, though she struggled, she was too weak to run away.

The heavens became dark and it began to rain. Thunder crashed and lightning flashed across the sky. It got darker and darker. The sea roared. Then an angry Ahai appeared at the house of the landlord.

Seeing his pitiful mother and fearing greatly for her safety, however, he agreed to the landlord's demand that he go to sea and fish. But Ahai never returned. His mother waited and waited for him at the top of Wang'Er Hill overlooking the sea. When she died, she turned into a stone that looks like an old woman keeping watch for her son.

历史

as told by
Zhu Shijie

A Tiger Saves a Beautiful Woman

I live in the city of Dalian. It is a well-known summer resort town, with beautiful hills, an alluring seashore, and an exceptional climate. There are also Xinghai and Baiyunshan parks, Tiger Strand amusement park, and Bangchui Island.

If you visit Dalian you will see a stone statue concerning a tale I learned as a child from the elderly woman next door. What is the story behind this statue? Let me tell you.

*L*ong, long ago, a big tiger lived in a cave by the seashore. Today no one knows exactly where the cave was, but in those days people knew that this tiger was not very fierce and was even somewhat friendly to the people in the area. Sometimes it was also mischievous; the tiger had the unusual power of controlling the level of the waters round the village. When fishermen were out in their boats, sometimes the tiger would strand them high and dry, and other times he would raise the sea level and fill their boats with water. Despite this, the villagers looked at the tiger as a friend of the people.

Some years later, a beautiful girl came to this village. When she went to the sea with her father, she would sing an enticing tune. The tiger was very fond of the song, so he made the sea calm when the girl was singing. Since the girl had come the sea was always calm and quiet, so the people were sure that it was her song that made the tiger gentle.

One day while the girl was fishing with her father and singing her beautiful song, the tiger became so excited that he started to dance on the sea, making the water rough and tipping the boat over. When the song suddenly stopped, the tiger realized what he had done. He felt very bad, so he lowered the water at once, saving the girl and her father from drowning. When the girl came to her senses, she was so frightened by her terrible experience that she decided to leave the village.

After she left the village, the tiger felt a twinge of conscience every time he thought of her. It was his own carelessness that had deprived the villagers of the girl and her beautiful song. What could he do? Should he go on with his reckless behavior, or should he do good deeds for the people? Being kind at heart, he decided on the latter. From that day on, the tiger helped the villagers whenever he could. Every day he told the villagers what the weather would be like and did his best to help them avoid accidents at sea, as well as bad storms. The people appreciated him very much and named a section of the beach Tiger Strand.

Many years passed and people put up a statue to honor the tiger. It is said that even today people can hear the tiger roaring in the night.

历史

as told by
Zhang Liwei

Zhaozhou Bridge

I come from an area not far from the city of Shijiazhuang, the capital of Hebei Province. There is a bridge in Hebei known as Zhaozhou Bridge. Today we know that Zhaozhou Bridge was built by Li Chun during the Sui Dynasty and that the traces told of in the story are marks left in an explainable way. Nevertheless, the story of how Lu Ban built this bridge has spread all over China, and this graceful, mythical tale has left a deep impression in people's minds.

The story is full of romantic color. It happened over two thousand years ago. I heard it from my grandmother, who has many interesting stories about Zhaozhou Bridge.

151

*L*ong, long ago, there lived a famous carpenter named Lu Ban. He did much ingenious work throughout his life. He is considered to be the father of Chinese carpentry because of his cleverness. For this reason there are many tales about Lu Ban.

In ancient Zhaozhou, floods often happened, especially in the Xiaohe River Basin. People there lived a hard life. To make matters worse, the Xiaohe River separated Zhaozhou into two. Even after the floods receded, traffic was still a problem. People on either side of the treacherous river could hardly go to the other side. They wanted someone to build a bridge over the Xiaohe River, but no one could. During this time of troubles, Lu Ban went there and, after seeing the people's difficult lives, resolved to help them. He was a carpenter, but this time he would build a stone bridge. Lu Ban began by building many small bridges on branches of the river. This made getting to the other side more convenient and less dangerous, though still slow.

Lu Ban knew that a bridge capable of withstanding the floods and rapid currents of the Xiaohe would have to be massive. Where would he find the proper stones? He searched for days without resting but found nothing. Exhausted and discouraged, he fell into a dream-filled sleep. In his dream he saw an old man with a snow-white beard driving a flock of sheep toward him from a distance. They came in front of him quickly. The old man smiled but did not say a word, then the man and his sheep all turned into snow-white stones.

When Lu Ban awoke, he was astonished to find the very stones he needed to build his bridge. With the materials he needed at hand, he and his men worked day and night, at last succeeding where no one had before. Seen from a distance, Zhaozhou Bridge looks grand, like a great dragon lying across the Xiaohe River or a majestic rainbow hung in the sky. As you approach the bridge you will find a stone dragon carved on its side and beautiful jade banisters.

The news of Lu Ban's great accomplishment spread quickly, and even the gods in heaven heard about it. Two gods who envied the people's respect for Lu Ban decided to create difficulties for him. One rode his donkey with three bags in which the sun, the moon, and the stars were loaded. The other followed, pushing a cart on which five great mountains sat. When they came across Lu Ban, they told him they did not believe that his bridge could support their donkey and cart until they saw it with their own eyes. Lu Ban just smiled as the two began to walk on the bridge. At every step a donkey's hoofprint and two wheel traces were left in the solid stone. As they rounded the top of the bridge, it started to shake from the immense weight upon it. Realizing what was happening, Lu Ban put out one of his own eyes[*] in frustration and anger.

Then, hoping to save his bridge, Lu Ban jumped underneath and began to support it with his own two bare hands. The huge bridge stopped shaking, but Lu Ban pressed so hard that the trace of his palm was left in the bridge. It is said that the traces of a donkey's hoof, a wheel, and a hand are clearly visible on the bridge.

[*] Legend has it that ever since then carpenters have used only one eye to sight a plumb line.

Lao Li Who Has No Tail

as told by
Qiu Xukui

I come from a small town, Dadian, near the city of Jinan in Shandong Province. It is well known that Shandong was not rich in the old days. Nowadays Shandong is acquiring a newfound prosperity, and, with plenty of factories and companies springing up, Shandong is becoming one of the richest provinces. Many peasants even own factories and live in pretty two-story houses. The Yimeng area where I live is also famous for its revolutionaries. Many of them helped to found the People's Republic of China.

I will tell you a folktale that my father told me when I was a little child. I recall that he told me many wonderful stories; he was more of a storyteller than my mother was.

*L*ong, long ago, in Dadian, there was a farmer named Li whose wife was about to give birth. The farmer was very excited, for he wanted to be a father. Finally his wife gave birth, not to a boy or a girl, but to a snake without a tail. Such a strange creature had never appeared before, and the couple were greatly shocked and they cried. But when they became calm and looked around, they found nothing. The snake had disappeared. Every year on that date, however, there was a big storm with plenty of much-needed rain. The people believed that the rain was caused by that little snake without a tail, Lao Li, named after his farmer father Li.

It was later said that Lao Li was a minister in heaven who had done something wrong, so he was sentenced by the King of Heaven to be born on earth as a snake without a tail. After his punishment was over, Lao Li was allowed to go back to heaven. He still remembered his hometown, and every year he visited it, bringing rain that was needed for the crops as a gift to the people.

For some years, there were no large storms in Dadian. Recently, however, there was a great storm, so it was said that Lao Li must have visited on that day.

历史

as told by
Zhang Chuyang

Lu Ban's Bet

I come from Hangzhou, Zhejiang. Hangzhou is best known for West Lake. Every year thousands of Chinese and foreign tourists come to the city to visit this beautiful lake. Hangzhou has a history over one thousand years long. Before the Ming Dynasty, it was called Lin'an and was the capital of the Southern Song Empire. Today there are over 2,000,000 people in Hangzhou, and it is developing into a modern city.

The story I will tell you takes place in Hangzhou. I heard it from my high school teacher.

*L*u Ban was one of the best craftsmen in all of China. One day Lu Ban and his younger sister were visiting West Lake in Hangzhou. The scenery was beautiful and they were enjoying it greatly, when suddenly they were caught in a downpour and had to return home.

"What a pity!" said sister Lu. "If there were some way to stay dry, we could enjoy the scenery in the rain."

When they reached home, sister Lu said to her brother, "You are the best craftsman around, but I'll make a bet with you. Let's see who can invent something that will allow people to enjoy the scenery, even in the rain."

Lu Ban was very interested and laughed. "All right, my dear sister," he said, "I'll accept your bet. But I think there must be a time limit. What about three days?"

"No," said sister Lu, "three days is too long. I think that one night is enough. We can start tonight and stop at the first rooster's crow tomorrow."

Lu Ban was very surprised by his sister's suggestion, but he said, "All right, it's a bet."

Because Lu Ban was the best craftsman in Hangzhou, it was very easy for him to build some wooden pavilions by the water. When it got dark, he began building some of these small shelters at the lakeshore so that people would be able to enjoy the scenery, even in bad weather. When he finished his first pavilion, Lu Ban went home and looked through the window of his sister's workshop. All was quiet inside. His sister had not yet begun to work. Lu Ban laughed and thought to himself, "It seems I will win the bet."

Lu Ban went back to the lakeshore and began to build another pavilion, then another, and still another. He built nine and started working on the tenth. Before he could finish the tenth, he heard a rooster crowing, so he stopped. Soon the sun rose. As he stood by one of the pavilions wondering what his sister had done, Lu Ban suddenly saw something coming toward him, something like the roof of a pavilion. Under it was his sister! As she came near, Lu Ban saw that she was holding a bamboo pole that had something round and flat at one end and was covered with silk of many colors.

"What a useful thing! How clever!" he cried out.

Sister Lu smiled and said, "Mine can only be used by a single person, while yours can be used by many at the same time. What's more, your pavilions gave me the idea. The scenery looks so much nicer from under your pavilions."

Some say that this was the beginning of the Hangzhou umbrella.

历史

as told by
Ling Zili

The Future Emperor's Death

I come from Shaoyang, Hunan. Hunan is in the southern part of China, and Shaoyang is in southwest Hunan.

In Shaoyang, there is a place where a boy who was predicted to become emperor was born. As it happened, he once had to escape being killed by soldiers of the man whom he was predicted to succeed as emperor. He was finally killed by this man. Near the place where he was born there is a stone which was used to step up onto a horse; it is said that the emperor-to-be stood on this very stone to mount his horse to escape.

My grandmother told me this story, which happened a long time ago.

*L*ong, long ago, there was a cruel emperor who had seers to predict the future. One day these men informed the emperor that there was a place where brilliant light shone through the clouds, which could only mean that a boy who would someday become emperor was to be born there. The emperor, fearing that the boy would one day replace him, decided to kill the boy before he could become a threat.

Without delay the emperor sent his most capable general and many soldiers to find and kill the boy. The boy was no ordinary lad, however, and, soon after his birth, he realized that he was in great danger. When the soldiers came near, he made ready to escape. As soon as he heard the sounds of the general's soldiers, he grabbed a large iron pot and put it over himself. Then he rushed out of the house, where he found a large wooden horse. Strangely, the wooden horse started to move toward the little boy, kneeling down to allow him to mount. However, the horse was still too high. Just as the soldiers arrived, a stone descended from the sky and landed exactly in the place for the boy to climb to mount the horse. In a moment the boy was on the horse.

The horse neighed loudly and began to run, leaving the soldiers far behind. Another group of soldiers headed them off and surrounded them. The boy used his iron pot for protection against the soldiers' arrows, while the horse ran as fast as he could to escape. After they had gone a long way, they reached a wide river, but the horse was able to jump in and swim across. Because it was wooden, the horse easily stayed afloat until they were safely on the opposite bank. Unfortunately, an enormous mountain now blocked their way, and, when they tried to go around it, they found even more of the emperor's men waiting for them.

This time they were truly surrounded, and escape looked most difficult. Soldiers were everywhere, and the emperor himself had come to watch the destruction of the boy. The soldiers set the mountain afire while the boy and his wooden horse rushed about looking for a way to escape. Finally the horse caught fire and began to burn. Surrounded, the boy tried to protect himself with the pot, but even that began to melt in the heat. Arrows flew from all directions. Suddenly, as the emperor approached, the boy spurted a great plume of fire that engulfed the emperor and all of his seers, killing everyone. In this way what the emperor had feared came true, though the boy did not become ruler as had been predicted.

历
史

as told by
Xu Xuemai

The Legend of the Duan Wu Festival

I come from Yueyang, Hunan. My home-town is a good place to live. It is beautiful, old, and modern all at once. Dongting Lake lies on one side of the city. Many rivers, including the Yangtze, flow into this lake.

In my hometown, the Duan Wu Festival is a special celebration. On May 5* every year, people eat *zongzhi,*** hang sweetgrass above their doors, and hold dragon boat races. How did these customs come into being? There is a legend about the festival, which is said to commemorate the great poet and patriot Qu Yuan. I have heard this legend about the Duan Wu Festival hundreds of times. Even today, children still hear this story from their grandmothers and grandfathers.

---

* According to the Chinese lunar calendar.
** A *zongzhi* is a pyramid-shaped dumpling made of glutinous rice, wrapped in bamboo or reed leaves.

*Q*u Yuan lived during the Warring States Period. He was born into an aristocratic family in the Chu Kingdom, which was then one of the seven most powerful kingdoms. When he was young, Qu Yuan received the best education and formed his idealism and patriotism. He made up his mind to serve the king and the people. He wished to make the kingdom richer and more powerful.

When he grew up, Qu Yuan was appointed to an important official post. His ability and wisdom, especially in diplomacy, were soon appreciated by the king. The king made him a minister and gave him more power. Qu Yuan worked very hard and considered all things carefully. During this time, most of the other officials began to respect him, and some envied him.

As Qu Yuan learned more than the others about the situation in the kingdom, he became worried. At that time, the Chu Kingdom was on good terms with the Qi Kingdom. The two kingdoms were neighbors and benefited from their good relations. On the other hand, the Qin Kingdom was their joint enemy and had designs on both the Chu and the Qi. Qu Yuan predicted disaster. He realized that if the slightest rift developed between the Chu and the Qi, the Qin would attack one and then the other. The situation was urgent and he set about warning the king.

Qu Yuan wrote a number of letters about this situation to the king, but the king disregarded them. In addition, Qu Yuan advised the king to cement his relations with the Qi and not to meet with the Qin. Again, the king ignored his advice. Instead he listened to his wife Zheng Xiu and an official named Jin Shang. Zheng Xiu was a cruel woman and hated Qu Yuan, while Jin Shang envied Qu Yuan. Together Zheng Xiu and Jin Shang collaborated with an envoy of the Qin, Zhang Yi, taking bribes and arranging for the king of Chu to meet with Zhang Yi. At their meeting, Zhang Yi asked the king to break off relations with the Qi and refuse to help the Qi if attacked by the Qin. In return, Zhang promised the king that he would get 500 li of land. The king of Chu was such a fool that he agreed to this deal.

Qu Yuan knew very well that this was all a trick to lure the Chu into war, but Jin Shang and Zheng Xiu told the king many false and damaging things about Qu Yuan. The king would not listen to Qu Yuan's warnings and even refused to meet with him. Qu Yuan became very sad, for he saw the Chu Kingdom heading toward destruction and the people's lives becoming worse. Not knowing what to do, he often got drunk and wrote poems.

While Qu Yuan was burning with anxiety about the kingdom, the king was feasting and dreaming. One day the king sent Qu Yuan into exile aboard a ship, ordering him to go south to barren lands. As the ship sailed away, Qu Yuan could not help looking back with tears in his eyes at his beloved country. The river was rough and the weather cold, and no crops could be seen on shore for the villagers. The nation suffered, but Qu Yuan could do nothing.

When Qu Yuan arrived at his destination, the people there came to welcome and encourage him. His landing place is very near to my hometown, Yueyang. Despite the hardships of his trip, he had managed to write many poems full of beauty and sweetness, which express in pure fashion the idealism and patriotism of his youth. In his exile, Qu Yuan became a very great poet and his poems came to be recited by people far and wide. Some of his students collected his works into two volumes, which helped to spread his fame. Even today, Qu Yuan's poems are still read and recited by many people.

Eventually the news came that the Chu Kingdom had been defeated by the Qin and that the king was in prison. Qu Yuan could not bear it and on May 5 he jumped into the Miluo River and committed suicide. The people searched for his body but could not find it. Legend has it that a big fish finally brought his body to shore. Though Qu Yuan was gone, the people knew that his spirit would not die, so they vowed to remember him every year on the day he died.

From then on, people dropped rice and zongzhi into the river. Now people all over China eat zongzhi on Duan Wu day. They also put *ai hao** over their doors, which is said to drive the evil spirits away. In my hometown, there is a special celebration, a large dragon-boat race. Teams come there from all over China and even from other parts of the world.

Though Qu Yuan belonged to the Chu Kingdom, he belongs to all of China today. He is worthy of deep respect.

---

* Ai hao is a kind of sweetgrass described in one of Qu Yuan's poems.

The Great Poet

as told by
Gui Qijun

My hometown is the city of Dantu in Anhui Province. It lies in the southeastern part of China. It has become an important industrial base, but hundreds of years ago it was beautiful countryside. The climate was warm and rainy, so the farmers who lived in this area grew mainly rice. Even today, lakes and brooks full of fish dot the land. Many years ago, people used boats to travel and to transport goods. Today ships are still widely used on the Changjian River, though they are bigger and speedier than before. My hometown has no high mountains, but it does have some very steep and beautiful hills.

When I was a child I often heard stories about my city, Dantu, but the one I remember best is about the great poet Li Bai.[*]

[*] Li Bai, Li Bo, and Li Po are all common spellings of the poet's name.

During the Tang Dynasty, there was a very talented poet named Li Bai. The city where he was born was in western China. In those days, the Tang Dynasty was very powerful, so his birthplace was at the far reaches of the country. When he was a young man, Li Bai was very bright, but not interested in reading. One day he met an old woman who was working hard to make a piece of steel into a needle. He watched until she finished her task. This taught him that only hard work can lead to success.

From then on, he read many books and became a gifted poet. It was not long before he attained a position in the emperor's court. Li Bai did well and his achievements were great. Because of his integrity and success, however, he was envied by many selfish men who spoke much evil about him before the emperor. Li Bai had no fear of them and only looked down upon them. One day, after he had drunk too much, he made the empress's brother carry his boots while he walked barefoot. He was dismissed from his position in the court and was forced to leave the capital.

Li Bai's first love was poetry, so after he left the court, he resolved to visit the many great mountains and rivers in China. During the course of his travels he wrote many poems. People said that he was fond of drinking, and that only when he was drunk could he write his best poems. Li Bai devoted most of his adult life to writing poems. Gradually he became so poor that he had almost no food to eat. Though he was known as a great poet, he refused to take money for his work from the rich, preferring to live the life of a drifter.

When he was nearly sixty years old, Li Bai became tired of wandering and decided to settle down. He set up a cottage beside the Yangtze River. He had little, but he was kind to the poor and continued to write poems without taking any money for them. Often he would visit his neighbors and ride in their boats. One evening he had drunk too much. The surface of the river was calm, and the full moon was hanging low in the sky. Li Bai suddenly became sad as he thought of his wasted youth and difficult life. Gazing into the river, he saw another moon as beautiful as the one in the sky. Diving into the water to grasp this moon, he drowned.

After his death, people realized what a great man they had lost. Though they buried him at the foot of Qi Mountain, many said that he could not die. They said instead that he was seen going away on a dragon.

历史

as told by
Sun Jianqui

Zhaojun

My hometown is Chifeng, Inner Mongolia. It lies in the eastern part of the province, and anyone in China will think of Inner Mongolia if you mention grasslands, milk, and the traditional Mongolian shelter, the *yurt*. Products made of milk are very popular, as well as beef and mutton. Chifeng also has many textile factories that export their products to America, Japan, and Europe.

In the history of our country, there are many outstanding women. Wang Zhaojun is one of them, and she is also one of the Four Beauties in Chinese history.

*W*ang Zhaojun was born during the Western Han Dynasty. At this time, there was a war for land between the Western Han and people in Inner Mongolia. The war went on for many years, and many people died on both sides. The Western Han wanted to stop the war, but no way could be found. A talented and brave young girl, Zhaojun suggested that the war could be stopped by intermarriage between the Han and the Mongolians, so she volunteered to marry the Mongolian prince. Her marriage stopped the fighting, and she devoted herself to reconciling the two nations.

After she died, people built many tombs, in different places, to honor this famous heroine. It is said that the grass on other tombs turns yellow in the autumn, while the grass on Wang Zhaojun's tomb stays green all year long. People call her burial place the Green Tomb. Many tombs in China are claimed to be Zhaojun's, though the one in Inner Mongolia is truly hers. As for the grass on Zhaojun's tomb, I do not know whether it is always green. You will know if you go to Inner Mongolia in the fall.

历史

as told by
Fanao Jun

The King's Daughter

*M*any people are familiar with the province of Sichuan because of restaurants serving Sichuan cuisine. Sichuan is also famous for its beautiful girls. High mountains, clear waters, and delicious food attract many tourists to my home province for vacations. People who know Sichuan also know the city of Chengdu. Because Chengdu is very clean and its climate is mild, it is a nice place to visit.

In addition to being a good place to spend a vacation, Sichuan has many interesting folktales. I will tell you one that deeply impressed me. I heard it from my grandmother.

*L*ong, long ago, Sichuan was a large plain, on which there was a kingdom. In this kingdom was a king who had only one daughter, whom he loved very much She liked running here and there, however, and often disappeared for many days. Each time this happened, the king was very worried because he never knew where she had gone.

One day an old man with a white beard gave the daughter a small fan that allowed her to fly through the air when she waved it. The king did not approve of this and ordered his guards to keep a close watch on the girl. But because she still had the mysterious fan, they could not keep her at home.

The king became more and more angry and tried to think of a way to keep his daughter at home. He thought and thought, and finally he came up with a solution. He sent many people to build a high wall around the kingdom, so high that the girl could not fly over it. The girl became sad and began to cry. Her tears became rivers, and the wall eventually became Sichuan's high mountains. This is why the province looks like a basin with very high mountains, and clear streams, rivers, and lakes.

历史

as told by
Li Yuan

Yee and the Nine Suns

I come from the city of Jiangyou in Sichuan Province. It is a rich and beautiful area called Heaven's Kingdom. Like other provinces, Sichuan has a very long history. There were several kingdoms founded there in ancient times, such as the Shu Kingdom during the Three Kingdom Period. Jiangyou, though small, is an old city. Li Bai, the famous poet of the Tang Dynasty, lived there for several years. Jiangyou is also known for Mount Tuan, which has a couple of iron chains hanging between two high peaks.

The people in Jiangyou have many old stories. When I was a child, I would often sit under a big tree listening to my grandfather or one of my sisters tell this story.

历史

as told by
Xu Aimin

The Liangshan Heroes and the Ginseng Celestial

*I*come from Changchun, Jilin, which lies to the north and east of Liaoning. Jilin Province is famous for its flourishing agriculture and its chemical and auto industries. In the western and central parts of the province, there are fertile plains. Beautiful Changbai Mountain is in the east. Jilin is also famous for many special products, ginseng being one of the most well known.

There are many folktales from this region, which have been handed down from generation to generation. When I was very young, my grandmother told me many interesting folktales about the Ginseng Celestial and other strange creatures. I can still remember some of them.

*O*nce upon a time, in a thickly forested part of Changbai Mountain, there lived a Ginseng Celestial who was over fifteen hundred years old. The mountaineers would often see a little boy in red, who went out every night to pay his respects to the Big Dipper and the moon. Then he would fly from one mountain to another just to pass the time. By day he would rest in the dense forest. The mountaineers tried many times to catch him, for they knew he was very valuable, but they never succeeded.

One year during the Song Dynasty, a war broke out between some Liangshan rebels and troops of the Song government. During one particularly fierce battle, a Liangshan general was hit with a poisoned arrow. Many medicines were tried to cure the general, but all failed. He was close to death when one of the doctors announced that he needed a bowl of one-thousand-year-old ginseng to make the medicine that would cure the general. Because there was no ginseng in southern China, the Liangshan commander ordered the brave Dai Jong, a soldier hero, to look for the ginseng in the far north. Another courageous man, Li Kui, volunteered to go with him. Being a great warrior and athlete, Dai could run over 500 miles per day. Li, however, could not, until Dai used his magic power to help him run faster and longer.

The two men sped across the land at an incredible speed, reaching Changbai Mountain in a short time. The mountaineers told them what the Ginseng Celestial looked like, but warned them that he was protected by a ferocious leopard. Unafraid, the two men quickly went into the thick forest. They found the Ginseng Celestial sitting on a big stone. Beside him was an enormous leopard, ready to protect him from any danger. Without hesitation, Li attacked the animal with a broad ax and slew it. Seeing this, the Celestial took to the air, and though Dai and Li kept up the chase until they were exhausted, they could not catch him.

By this time the commander of the Song Army had nearly lost hope, as the general was almost dead. When everyone thought all was lost, a military counselor named Wu Yong spoke up, saying, "Please let us try again. This time I will go with Dai."

The commander agreed to let them try again. This time, however, they would try a different strategy. They began by making seven small lanterns and a large one, then arranged them in the form of the Big Dipper and the moon. As it happened to be a dark night, only the lanterns were visible. Wu and Dai hid and waited silently.

After a while, something became visible in the northwest sky. As they watched, it slowly approached. Through the air flew a plump little boy, riding a red-tinted gust of wind. The Ginseng Celestial headed straight for the lanterns, thinking that they were the moon and Big Dipper. As he bowed down before the lanterns, Wu rushed out and shouted, "Wooden club!" The Celestial was so frightened that he tried to run away, but he seemed to be held fast by some magic power. The poor little Celestial kneeled and begged for mercy, promising to give the two men whatever they wanted if only they would let him go. "You know I am over fifteen hundred years old," he cried out.

The two men assured him that they would not kill him. They only wanted to ask for a little help. When they told the Celestial the trouble they were in, he agreed without hesitation to help them. He stretched out one arm. Wu took out a knife and cut an opening. No sooner had he done this than a bright white fluid began to drop from the wound, soon filling a small bowl. Meanwhile, the Ginseng Celestial turned sallow and emaciated-looking, but he told them that he might regain his strength after another five hundred years or so. Then he waved good-bye and flew away.

Wu and Dai went back to Liangshan immediately. The doctor made up a prescription with the ginseng juice, then helped the wounded general to drink it. Soon the general regained his health and lived to fight again.

历史

as told by
Liu Bing

Sun and Moon

I was born in Nanning, Guangxi, but I consider Guilin to be my hometown. It is the city that is said to have the best scenery in all of China. Guangxi has many ethnic minorities that have their own customs and languages. Until I went to school at age six, I lived with my grandmother, who lived in Guangxi all her life. After she had finished her work, she would often tell me several folktales. Now that time has passed, I can only remember some of them. The following is one of the ones I can recall.

*L*ong, long ago, there were two suns in the sky. They were like two very large, heated balls that made the land so hot that people did not dare to go out and work. Because of this, they could not make a living. One day a young man named Tongzi, whose head was made of iron and his body of steel, decided to bring the suns under control. He had a bow that weighed 8,888 kilograms and could shoot anything nearer than 55,555 kilometers away.

At first Tongzi was eager to shoot the suns quickly, but, as he approached them, the heat made him so sick that he could not even lift his bow. The next time he tried to shoot them, he stayed far enough away that the heat did not harm him. He fired arrows with his heavy bow for forty-nine days, but none of his arrows struck their target. The suns nevertheless became so scared that they hid in the mountains, causing the sky and land to become dark.

The people still could not make a living, so Tongzi found the two suns and ordered one to come out during the day and the other at night. The suns obeyed, and people called the one that came out during the day "sun" and the one that came out at night "moon."

From that time on, the sun served the people faithfully and was praised by them, but the moon fairy met a sky-dog* who was moved by her beauty and wanted to catch her. She had to ask Tongzi for help. Although his arrows had been used up in his fight with the suns, he promised to try to help her.

He thought for eighty-one days and finally came up with a good idea. He asked the moon fairy to hide in the clouds during the day so as not to be found by the sky-dog. Then he asked the people to get some *shizi*** and make it into round, sweet cakes. At night when the people threw the cakes into the sky, the sky-dog thought that they were the moon fairy and ran towards them. In this way the moon fairy was able to get free of the sky-dog, so she could come out of the clouds to bring light to the people at night.

---

* The sky-dog may be a constellation in the Chinese night sky.
** Shizi is a kind of fruit.

历
史

as told by
Cui Binghui

Chen Xiang Chopped the Mountain

I was born in Shuaxian County in Shaanxi Province. The capital of Shaanxi, Xi'an, is very famous for the thousands of terra-cotta warriors that were found there in the tomb of Emperor Qin Shihuangdi in 1974. Xi'an was the capital of many dynasties, including the Qin and the Tang. Today, in addition to its long and rich history, Xi'an is also a thriving economic center.

In Shaanxi's Huayin County there is a famous holy mountain, called Huashan. If you climb the mountain, you will find a golden axe standing to the side of a narrow path in front of a large crack in the rock. There is a popular story about this crack that I would like to tell you.

*L*ong, long ago, a young man lived near Huashan Mountain. This man was very handsome and intelligent, but he was an orphan and very poor. In spite of this, he studied hard, seldom leaving his books each day. A fairy in heaven was moved by his dedication, so she flew down to earth to become his wife, giving him a beautiful piece of jade as proof of her love. After a few years, she gave birth to a baby boy, whom they named Cheng Xiang.

When their marriage and the birth of their child became known to the fairy's brother, he became angry, feeling that it was a disgrace for a fairy from heaven to marry a human being. He went to earth, intending to carry his sister back to heaven.

The couple had no idea that this was going to happen. The fairy's brother was much stronger than his sister, so when he arrived, she had no choice but to follow him back to heaven. Her brother then locked her up inside Huashan Mountain. As a result of losing his wife, the young man died of grief.

Fortunately there was an affectionate old spirit named Taishanglao Jun, who took it upon himself to bring up little Cheng Xiang. Unhappy about what the fairy's brother had done to her and her husband, the old spirit taught the boy many useful things he would later be able to use.

As time went by, little Cheng Xiang grew into a strong young man. The old spirit gave Cheng Xiang a golden axe and asked him to rescue his mother from imprisonment in Huashan Mountain. Cheng Xiang went to the mountain, chopped a hole in its side with the axe, and saved his mother. Ever since then, Huashan Mountain has had this crack in its side.

Fairy Tales and Fables

神话

The Origin of Mount Qian

as told by
Song Zhihua

I come from the city of Anshan in Liaoning Province. Anshan is about two hours by train from the city of Shenyang. To most people, Anshan is well known for iron and steel. There are several flourishing commercial streets with a lot of elegant goods, as well as some nice parks. There are also a lake and hills just outside of town.

Qianshan is in the suburbs of Anshan. It is called the "first mountain of Liaoning Province," and there are a lot of temples there. Every spring many people come here to attend the Pear Flower Festival, but visitors arrive all through the year.

Over the years my grandfather told me many folktales. The story I will tell is one of them.

*A*bout two thousand years ago, a man lived in a beautiful village. He was brave, hard-working, handsome, and kind to everyone. A lotus-flower fairy saw this and decided to descend from heaven and live with the man. She took her pagoda with her and went to earth. They married and led a happy life together, until the Emperor of Heaven found out about what they had done and became very angry. Wanting to punish them, he sent guards to capture the fairy and kill the man.

The fairy, however, discovered the emperor's plans. Wasting no time, she took out her pagoda, which showered forth lotus flowers that turned into mountains, each having its own size and shape. There were 999 of them. When the Emperor of Heaven's guards arrived in the small town, the couple had already gone into the mountains and hidden themselves. The guards ran after them but quickly lost their way in the many gullies, because it was very difficult to distinguish the path.

The guards searched for some time without success and finally returned to heaven dejectedly. The emperor was greatly shocked by their report and made up his mind to go by himself at night. The couple were not prepared for his coming, so they were caught at once. In spite of the fairy's pleas and the man's explanations, the emperor took out his sword and stabbed the man. Blood gushed out of his body and he fell down, dead. Thought the fairy was broken-hearted and tears ran down her cheeks, she pretended to agree to go back to heaven with the emperor. First, however, she must bury her husband. She did this tearfully, then broke free from the guards and knocked on a large stone nearby. Immediately she began to change and turned into the mountain we now call Qianshan, making the total number of mountains 1,000, no less and no more.

Though the fairy passed away long ago, she left this beautiful mountain for us to enjoy.

神话

as told by
Yang Ming

Phoenix Mountain

My hometown is a small city named Dandong, which is in Liaoning Province. Dandong is quiet and clean, and the weather is nice. If you want to go swimming, the Yalu River is a good place to go. Along the river is a park where you can walk, with colorful flowers and green trees. Over the river there are two bridges. One is no longer used, because it was partially destroyed during the Korean War. The other bridge is newer and is used to cross over to North Korea. Dandong is famous not only for its scenery, but also for its silk.

When I was a little girl, my grandfather used to tell me many wonderful stories. One about Phoenix Mountain impressed me so much that even now I remember it clearly.

*L*ong, long ago, there was a high mountain without a name. No one wanted to live near it because there were so many wild animals on it, but at the foot of the mountain was a hunter who lived with his aged mother. In order to make a living, every morning the hunter went to the mountain and came back in the afternoon with small animals, such as rabbits and foxes. In this way many years passed.

One day, it was very cold. Because he did not have anything to eat, the hunter went to the mountain. When he got to the mountain he was very puzzled, because everything was not as it had been. There were no birds singing or monkeys playing; it was so quiet that he felt some terrible thing had happened. Just as he was going to go back, he caught sight of a beautiful bird that he had never seen before. He raised his bow and aimed it at the bird. As he was about to shoot it, he saw a tear roll down from one of the bird's eyes. Shocked, he slowly lowered his bow and turned toward home.

On his way home, he came upon a beautiful girl who had fallen into a river. He jumped into the water and saved her, then he asked her who she was and why she was there. She told him that her parents had died and that she had no way to make a living. The hunter was very kind, so he took her home with him. His mother was pleased with the girl, because she was soft-hearted and diligent. One year later, with the blessing of the young man's mother, the two got married. They lived happily, for they loved each other deeply. They thought of themselves as the happiest couple on earth. But how long could such happiness last?

One cold day five years later, the young lady was very sad. When her husband asked her what troubled her, she began to cry and said, "Do you remember the beautiful bird that you saved in the forest? It was a phoenix."

"A phoenix?" asked the young man.

"Yes," replied the girl. "I am that phoenix you saved. Five years ago, a large tiger ran loose on the mountain scaring and killing many of the animals there. They came to me for help. I fought the tiger and scared it away, but I was hurt. I would have had no way to defend myself if you had decided to shoot me with your bow and arrow. But you were a kind-hearted man and left me unharmed. For this, I was deeply moved and turned into a young woman and came to live with you.

"Now there is another tiger in the forest and the animals in the woods need help. But if I turn back into a phoenix to fight the tiger, I cannot return to you as a girl. Although you are strong, the tiger is too big for you to kill, so I must go myself. Will you remember me when I am gone? I won't forget you."

After saying this, she disappeared. The hunter was amazed. He could not believe his eyes and ears. He picked up his bow and arrows and ran straight for the mountain, where he saw the beautiful phoenix battling a ferocious tiger. He drew his bow and shot the tiger, which was wounded and ran away.

The phoenix looked at the hunter for a long time, then tears again came into her eyes. Slowly, she turned and flew away.

The hunter stood quietly, not crying but sad at heart. He made up his mind never to kill any bird again. Then he went back home, alone.

This is how the beautiful mountain near Dandong came to be called Phoenix Mountain.

神
话

as told by
Yao Ming

Small Sweep and the Wolf

*B*enxi, my hometown, is a city 100 kilometers east of Shenyang, the capital of Liaoning Province. Benxi's economy is primarily centered around heavy industry.

Surrounded by mountains, Benxi is sometimes called Mountain City, and it is also traversed by the Taizi River. In and around Benxi, there are a number of interesting places to see. Benxi Water Cave is said to be one of the biggest of its kind in Asia, while Benxi Lake is the smallest lake in the world. In addition, there are Tiecha, Guanmen, and Wunu mountains, Wanxi Park, Huairen Reservoir, and Dripping Cave.

Twenty years ago, my grandmother told me a story about a family and a wolf.

*L*ong, long ago, a mother and her three sons, named Big Bolt, Second Bolt, and Small Sweep, lived in a small village. Around this village was a forest in which there were many wolves.

One day they received a message from a neighbor that their grandmother was ill and wanted very much for her daughter to come. The mother worried about the grandmother, so she decided to go see her. Before she left, she said to her three sons, "My sons, I'm going to see your grandma. Because there are so many wolves around this village who often kill and eat people, you must stay at home. Do not open the door until I come home. When I come back, I will say, 'Big Bolt, Second Bolt, and Small Sweep, open the door.' Unless you hear those exact words, do not open the door. There might be some bad man or a wolf who has come to do you harm. Do you hear what I say, my sons?"

"Yes, mother," the boys answered.

After the mother had prepared food for her sons and herself, she left for the grandmother's house.

As the mother was speaking her final words to her sons, however, there was a wolf outside the door who heard everything she said. He knew that the woman would soon set out, leaving her three sons in the house.

When the mother left the house, the wolf followed her into the woods. After she had gone a ways, the wolf killed her by biting her throat and ate her.

One evening a few days later, the wolf put on the mother's clothes and kerchief and knocked at the door of the house. Making his voice sound like the mother's, he said, "Big Bolt, Second Bolt, Small Sweep, open the door." The boys thought that their mother had come back, so they opened the door quickly.

The wolf entered the room, saying, "My sons, don't light the fire. I'm very tired. Let's go to bed." Once again he made his voice sound like the mother's and the room was very dark, so the boys suspected nothing. They went to sleep.

In the middle of the night, when the boys were asleep, the wolf bit the throat of Big Bolt and ate him. Small Sweep woke up, and, hearing the sound of eating, he asked, "Mother, what are you eating?"

"Your grandma knew that I have a cough, so she gave me some radish," replied the wolf.

Small Sweep said, "Mother, may I please have a piece of radish?"

The wolf gave him one of Big Bolt's fingers. Small Sweep almost cried out, but kept silent out of fear. Then, touching the wolf's body and finding it all furry, he asked, "Mother, why is there fur all over your body?"

The wolf was surprised and answered, "Your grandma knew that I was cold, so she gave me a fur coat."

By now Small Sweep knew that it was a wolf, not his mother, in the house. He quietly climbed into the attic, hung a hook from one of the beams, and wrapped it with meat. Then he shouted, "Mother, we bought a piece of meat for you. Would you like it?"

The wolf was very excited when he heard this, so he climbed up to the attic to get the piece of meat. He swallowed the meat, catching his mouth on the hook. Small Sweep rushed over and beat the wolf on the head until he was dead.

In this way, though his mother and Big Bolt had been killed, Small Sweep saved himself and Second Bolt from being eaten by the wolf.

神话

as told by
Yin Yufang

Seven Fairies

My hometown, Shiyan, lies in the middle of China, in Hubei Province. The hills around Shiyan are covered with green grass and all kinds of trees and wildflowers. When spring comes, it is beautiful. Shiyan itself is an industrial city, with a big factory that produces automobiles. In the summer the weather is hot, and in the winter it is cold. Sometimes it snows and everything turns white. Near the city is a mountain that is holy to Taoists, with many ancient buildings still standing.

I will tell a story I heard from my grandmother, a kind old woman. I always wished that the story had ended happily. The events of this story happened long, long ago.

*I*t is said that in heaven there were supernatural beings who lived happily and never knew the kind of troubles humans suffer. They had magic weapons and could appear and disappear mysteriously.

One day seven fairy sisters were playing in a park in heaven. They were a little tired and began to talk. One of the sisters said, "I wish I knew what the earth was like."

Another said, "Me, too. But father and mother won't let us go down to earth. I've heard that it is very beautiful there."

The littlest one said suddenly, "Why don't we go secretly? We can go down for a while just to see what it's like. If none of us tells, no one will find out. Okay?"

"Good idea!" the other sisters shouted.

The eldest girl made no answer. All the sisters turned to her, waiting for her to think it over. Finally she agreed, so they flew off into the sky and down to the earth below.

Once they were down on earth, they were attracted by what they saw. They were delighted by all of the new and wonderful things. They flew all about excitedly. Soon the littlest sister spied a handsome man by a well. He was a cowherd who worked for a landlord. What a pity! The young man had no parents, and every day he had to work and work. Seldom did he have enough food to eat or a warm place to sleep. The little fairy was touched by his hardships, so she made up her mind to help him.

At first she used her magic wand to help him collect firewood. The young man did not know what was happening, but after several days he decided to try to discover who was gathering wood for him. One day he pretended to leave home and hid himself behind the door. When the pretty little fairy girl appeared, he caught her by the arm and asked her to stay with him. Because she liked the young man very much, the fairy girl smiled and agreed.

When the other sisters gathered to go back to heaven, their little sister was missing. They looked everywhere and finally found her in the house of the cowherd. Though they tried their hardest to persuade her to go back, she would not, for she loved the young man very much. Finally the sisters went back without her.

The couple worked hard but they were happy. Alas, the fairies' father was angry that the girl had disobeyed him and went to earth to fetch her. Though the young man tried to follow them to heaven, he could not because he was merely a mortal. The girl's father forbade her to return to earth. The young man waited and waited for her in vain, and their story ends sadly.

The Story of the Snake

as told by
Zhang Yan

*I*come from Henan, a province in the central part of China. It has the second-largest population in China. On top of Song Mountain in Henan lies the famous Shaolin Temple, and the Yellow River also runs across Henan. The city where I live, Anyang, lies in the northern part of Henan. It is one of the oldest cities in China, and ever since it was founded it has been an important city. The famous national hero Yue Fei was born there. It also has many scenic spots, such as Leifeng Tower and the Heng River. To the west stands Nine Dragon Mountain. Anyang is a beautiful city and I love it very much.

The story I am going to tell I heard when I was a little boy. One day my father took me to his friend's home, where I was told a tale about a snake.

*O*ne day a snake lay in the sun at the foot of a mountain. The sun was warm and the snake fell asleep. Suddenly, however, a large rock came loose and rolled down the mountain, trapping the snake so that he could not move. The snake lay under the stone for many hours, afraid that no one was going to come and help him. He tried to get loose, but the stone lay across his back and kept him imprisoned.

Finally a rabbit came around the mountain. He was happy as he went through the grass in the warm sunshine. Then he saw the snake under the stone and stopped to speak to him.

"Good morning, Mr. Snake," said the rabbit. "Do you enjoy sitting under that stone?"

"Don't pull my leg," said the angry snake. "This stone is hurting me. Move it off me and I'll give you a reward."

The rabbit knew that the snake was unfriendly and dangerous, but the rabbit was kind-hearted and did not like to see other animals in pain. He slowly approached the stone.

"All right, I'll move it," the rabbit said. He tried to pick up the stone, but it was too heavy. He pushed on one side, then the other. At last he was able to move the heavy stone off the snake. The snake was free again, and the rabbit was very tired.

"Now I will give you your reward," said the snake.

"Oh, no, thank you," said the rabbit. "I don't want a reward. I just want to go home now. You should move out of the sun, too."

"It's a nice reward," said the snake.

"What is it?" asked the rabbit.

"You helped me," said the snake, "so now I'll eat you for my dinner."

"No, no," cried the rabbit, "that's not a reward! Please don't eat me, Mr. Snake! I'm too tired to run away from you."

"Yes, yes," said the snake, "I must have my dinner."

Just then a dog came around the mountain. "What's happening here?" he asked.

Both the rabbit and the snake began to talk at the same time. "You can be our judge," they said.

"What happened?" the dog asked.

"I came here and found Mr. Snake under the stone," the rabbit said. "He couldn't move, so I pushed the stone off him. He said he would give me a reward, but now he wants to eat me for his dinner. He says that's my reward."

"That's not true," the snake said. "I was under the stone, that part is true. But I always sleep under a stone. I don't like the hot sun. Mr. Rabbit pushed the stone and wanted to kill me. Now I want to eat him as his punishment."

The dog put his chin in his paw and looked at both the rabbit and the snake. Then he said slowly, "My friends, you agree that Mr. Snake was under the stone, don't you?"

"Yes," both the rabbit and the snake said. "That's true."

"Well," said the dog, "I must see you as you were, Mr. Snake. Please lie by the stone again. Mr. Rabbit and I will put it on top of you. Then I'll understand who is telling the truth."

The snake agreed. The rabbit and the dog put the stone back on top of him.

"Now," said the dog. "Is this how you were?"

"Yes," said the snake. "This is how I was."

"Can you move?" asked the dog.

"No," replied the snake.

"Then you must stay under the stone, and Mr. Rabbit can go home to his family."

神
话

as told by
Cao Mingke

The Well of the World's End

*A*nyang is my hometown and is in the northern part of Henan Province. It is a beautiful city. It was the capital of China about 3,000 years ago, and it is one of the seven ancient capitals. Many shell writings and other cultural relics have been found there. Industry in Anyang is developing very quickly now, and many modern factories have been built.

There is a well called the Well of the World's End in the suburbs of Anyang. Many stories about this well are still told today. This particular one was told by an elderly man who was one of my neighbors.

*O*nce upon a time, there was a girl called Lianhua. She was a good girl but not very clever, and a merry girl but not too pretty. All would have been well with her except that she had a cruel stepmother. Instead of having pretty dresses to wear, sweet cakes to eat, and idle friends to play with, as all girls should, Lianhua was made to do housework, to scrub the stone floors on her knees, and to roll up her sleeves to the elbows to do the washing. The better she did her work, the more her stepmother hated her. If she got up early in the morning, it was not early enough; if she cooked the dinner, it was not cooked right. Poor Lianhua! She worked all day, yet everything she did was wrong.

One day her stepmother decided to get rid of her. "Child," she said, "take this sieve and go to the Well of the World's End. When you have found it, fill the sieve with water and bring it back to me. Mind now, and see that you don't spill a drop. Be off with you!"

Lianhua, who never dared to talk back to her stepmother nor even to ask a question, took the sieve and went out to look for the Well of the World's End. When Lianhua told others what she wanted to do and asked where the well was, everyone laughed at her and told her that she was stupid and that there was no such well.

She continued on her search. At last she spied a ragged old woman, bent nearly double, looking for something in a cart-rut. She had a torn bonnet and hardly any teeth at all. She was poking in the mud with a crooked stick.

"What are you looking for?" asked Lianhua.

"I had two groats,* and if I don't find them I won't have anything to eat tonight."

Lianhua helped the old woman look for her groats, and presently her sharp eyes caught sight of them.

"Thank you," said the old woman in her creaky voice. "I would never have found them by myself, I do declare. Now tell me where you are going and what you are doing with that sieve."

"I'm going to the Well of the World's End," said Lianhua, "but I'm afraid there is no such place in the world. When I get there, I must fill this sieve with water and take it home to my stepmother."

"Why, indeed," said the old woman, "there is a Well of the World's End, and I'll tell you how to find it. As for what you are going to do when you get there, that's another matter."

---

* A groat is a coin worth a few pennies.

Pointing with her stick, she showed Lianhua the way. Lianhua thanked her and went in the direction the old woman had shown her. She came to a deep valley, all wet underfoot and very green and lonesome. At the very end of the valley was a well. It was so overgrown with ivy and moss that she nearly missed it. But there it was, sure enough, and this was the Well of the World's End.

Lianhua knelt down on the bank beside the well and dipped her sieve into the water. Many times she dipped it into the water, but each time the water ran through the holes in the sieve, with not a drop left to take back home to her stepmother. She sat down and cried.

"I'll never do it," she sobbed. "I'll never have a sieve full of water to take home."

Just as she was beginning to think that her misery would never end, something croaked and a fat green frog hopped out from under a fern leaf.

"What's the matter?" asked the frog.

Lianhua told him what her stepmother had ordered her to do.

"If you promise," said the frog, "to do everything I ask for a whole night, I can help you."

"Yes, of course I will," said Lianhua eagerly. "I'll promise whatever you like. Only do help me, please."

The frog considered for a moment and spoke:

"Stop it with moss, and daub it with clay
And then it will carry the water away."

Lianhua quickly gathered soft, green moss from the mouth of the well and covered the bottom of the sieve with it. Then she scooped up some damp clay from the bank and spread it on top of the moss, pressing it down until all of the holes in the sieve were filled. Then she dipped the sieve into the water, and this time not a drop ran out.

"I must get home as quickly as I can," she said, turning to go. "Thank you, dear frog, for helping me. I would never have thought of that myself."

"No, I don't suppose you would have," croaked the frog. "Carry the water carefully. And don't forget your promise."

Lianhua remembered that she had promised the frog that she would do anything he wanted for a whole night. She did not suppose that any harm would come of a promise made to a frog, so she told him that she would not forget and went on her way.

You can imagine how surprised her stepmother was to see her when she got home. The stepmother had hoped to get rid of the girl for good, but here she was, none the worse for the journey and carrying a sieve full of water, just as she had been told. The stepmother did not say much, because she was too angry for words. Instead, she made Lianhua make supper for them both and wash clothes afterwards, as if nothing had happened.

As night was falling, they were surprised to hear someone knocking at the door.

"Who can it be?" asked the stepmother.

Lianhua went to the door and asked, "Who is that, and what do you want at this time of night?"

There was a little croaking noise. "Open the door and let me in."

It was the frog. Lianhua had almost forgotten him. Her stepmother asked who was at the door, and Lianhua told her all about the frog and the promise she had made him.

"Well, let him in," said the stepmother, "and do as he tells you. Girls must keep their promises." She rather liked the idea of her stepdaughter having to obey the commands of a frog.

Lianhua opened the door, and the frog hopped in. He looked at her and spoke again, saying, "Lift me up to your knee."

Lianhua did not like the idea very much, but her stepmother said, "Do as he tells you. Girls must keep their promises."

The girl lifted the frog up. He sat perched on her knee and said, "Give me something to eat and drink."

"Do as he tells you," ordered the stepmother again. "Girls must keep their promises."

Lianhua fetched the food left over from supper and put it on a plate in front of the frog. He bent down his head and ate every scrap of it. Once more he spoke, saying "Take me into your bed."

"No," said Lianhua, "I will never have such a cold, clammy creature in bed with me. Get away, you nasty animal!"

At this the stepmother almost screamed with laughter. "Go on!" she cried. "Do as the frog bids. Remember your promise. Young girls must keep their promises."

With that the stepmother went off to her room, and Lianhua was left with the frog. She finally got into bed, taking the frog in beside her but keeping him as far away from her as she could. After a while she slept soundly.

In the morning, before the break of day, she was awakened by a croaking sound close to her ear.

"You have done everything I have asked," said the frog. "Do one more thing and you will have kept your promise. Take an axe and chop off my head!"

Lianhua looked at the frog, and her heart went cold. "Dear frog," she said, "don't ask me to do that. You have been so kind to me. Please don't ask me to kill you."

"Do as I ask," said the frog. "Remember your promise. The night is not yet over. Fetch an axe and chop off my head."

Very sadly Lianhua went into the kitchen and fetched a chopper that was used to cut up logs for the fire. She could hardly bear to look at the poor frog, but somehow she managed to raise the chopper and cut off his head.

Then she had the greatest surprise of her life. For the frog was no more, and in his place stood a handsome young man. She stepped back in amazement, dropping the axe to the floor. The young man was smiling at her.

"Don't be afraid," he said in a soft, musical voice. "I'm not here to hurt you. I was once a prince, but an evil enchantress turned me into a frog. Her wicked spell could not be broken until a young girl did my bidding for a whole night."

At that moment the stepmother, who had been awakened by the sound of voices, came into the room. Great was her astonishment to see the young prince there instead of the frog.

"Ma'am," said the prince, "your daughter has had the kindness to break the spell that made me a frog; for that I'm going to marry her. I'm a powerful prince, and you cannot deny me. You wanted to get rid of your stepdaughter. Well, your wish has come true, for now I'm going to take her away to be my wife."

For once the stepmother had nothing to say. She looked at the prince and opened her mouth, but no words came out. Then she looked at Lianhua and opened her mouth again, but still no words came. The only thing she could do was to turn away and begin to make some breakfast for them.

Not long afterwards the prince and Lianhua were married, and very happy they were.

A Saga

as told by
Sunzhao Xu

I come from the province of Shandong, in which there is a famous mountain called Mount Tai. My hometown, Laiwu, lies at the foot of it. On top of the mountain, you can see the famous sunrise of Mount Tai. From under a lot of white clouds, the red sun pops out like the face of a child. The sky turns red, then yellow, then blue. Mount Tai is a wonderful place to spend a vacation.

The following story was told to me by my grandmother.

*O*nce, long ago, the king of Kao had a daughter called Xiafei, who was fifteen years old, very sweet, and gentle. The king and his daughter loved each other dearly, for the king had no wife and his daughter had no mother, as she had died ten years earlier. Being not very wealthy and needing money, he finally married a rich woman who was ugly, ill-tempered, and spiteful. This rich woman had a daughter the same age as Xiafei. Unlike the beautiful Xiafei, however, she was plain, spiteful, and surly like her mother.

No sooner had the spiteful queen and her daughter settled down than they began to turn the king's mind against his daughter. At last Xiafei became so unhappy that she told her father that she must go out into the world and seek her fortune. The king could do nothing, though he loved her deeply. Resolved to see her go, the king told her, "You'll well be able to look after yourself."

He also instructed Xiafei to ask her stepmother to give her provisions for the journey. The queen, however, gave her nothing but a coarse bag of sacking containing dry bread and a small bottle of ale. She was glad that Xiafei was going away and did not care what became of her. Xiafei bade her father good-bye and set off to make her fortune.

Through the fields and woods she went, sad at heart. Soon she happened upon an old man sitting by the roadside. The old man asked her for something to eat. Xiafei sat with him and they had dinner together. The kind old man gave her a wand and told her that it would be useful if she crossed a thick thorn hedge. Xiafei continued on her way, and she went through a thick thorn hedge without any trouble.

After a while, she came to a well. From it arose the sound of voices and singing. Xiafei bent to look down, finding three heads with dirty hair. Their mouths opened and sang, "Wash me and comb me, and lay me down gently, that I may be comely for passers to see." Xiafei sat down beside the well and took the heads gently in her lap. With the cloth that covered her own head, she wiped their faces softly; with her comb she smoothed their wet, tangled hair. Then she placed them on a bank of primroses.

The three heads were glad and thankful. They promised Xiafei three presents. First, they would give her the gift of beauty and told her that a great king would take her for his wife. Second, they would give her a sweet voice, so that people would long to hear her songs. Third, they would give her riches, so that she would have something to give to the man who wed her. Then they asked Xiafei to put them back in the well.

Xiafei went on her way, singing and dancing. After a while, she met a handsome king in a beautiful forest. The king was attracted to her beauty and her sweet voice. The king instantly fell in love with her, and they were married soon afterward. The old sack given to her by her stepmother was by now full of diamonds, pearl necklaces, and other jewels, so Xiafei and her husband had all the money they wanted. They had a good life together.

One day they wanted to see Xiafei's father, so they went to visit him. Great was the ugly stepmother's surprise to see Xiafei and her handsome husband. And how delighted the king of Kao was! The queen was even more angry and jealous when she saw how beautiful Xiafei had become, how handsome and noble her husband was, and how rich and happy they both were. She determined to get such a husband for her daughter, ugly and spoiled as she was.

At the next meal they all sat together. Xiafei told her father and stepmother the whole story of the old man and the three heads in the well, as well as how she had met her husband. The next day, the queen took a fine, soft leather bag and filled it with delicate cakes and a bottle of the best wine. She gave it to her daughter, wished her good fortune, and sent her on her way.

Soon the ugly daughter met the old man, but she did not want to eat with him. Then she came upon a thick thorn hedge, and, when she tried to pass through it, she was badly cut and scratched. Covered with blood and scratches, she struggled to get out on the other side. After that, she came upon the same three heads with dirty hair in the well, but she did not want to clean and comb them. They promised her an unpleasant disease and a bad voice. At the end of her journey, she married a villainous-looking cobbler with a squint.

When the ugly daughter and her cobbler husband came back to visit her mother and stepfather, the queen could hardly speak for anger and spite. She soon fell ill and died of rage and grief. Nevertheless, the king of Kao took pity on the pair, giving them some money and asking them to go as far as they could to make a living. From then on, the king of Kao, Xiafei, and her husband led good, long, and happy lives.

神话

as told by
Yu Peilan

The Sea Fairy

I was born in a small village near the coastal city of Weihai. Both of my parents are peasants. Our village is surrounded by mountains, like a baby lying in its cradle. The climate of Shandong Province is moderate, not too cold in the winter and not too hot in the summer. Many people come to Weihai for sunbathing and swimming, and the people of our region are simple but friendly. Weihai has only light industry, so the air and streets are clean. In my region of China, many people make their living by farming or fishing. Lately, conditions have improved greatly.

Weihai is by the water, so there are many tales about the sea. I will tell you one of these stories. I heard it from my grandmother when I was a child.

203

*O*nce there was a man named Long Jun, who lived in the fields by the sea. Each day he drove his mother's cows out to the fields to graze on the grass.

One day, as he went along he said, "How cold it is, and how sad the fields look today!" Then he turned and looked at the sea. The sun came out and he saw a rock in the sea. A beautiful woman wearing a golden dress was sitting on the rock. "I've never seen anyone so beautiful," Long Jun said.

He wanted very much to hear her speak, so he took out the bread he had with him. He called to he woman, "I'm Long Jun! I want to talk to you. Will you come out of the water and share my lunch with me?"

The woman stood up, and Long Jun thought, "She's coming here! I will see her up close, hear her talk, and maybe even touch that beautiful golden dress!"

She came out of the sea to Long Jun. She looked at the bread that he offered her and said, "Your bread is too hard for me, much too hard. You can't give me such hard bread. I can't eat that bread." Then she went back into the sea.

Long Jun went home. He told his sad story to his mother. She loved her son very much and wanted him to be happy.

"That bread was too hard," she said. "I think I can make nice bread for you, bread that the fairy will like. You go to bed. I'll make some good bread for you. In the morning you can take the new bread out to the fields with you."

When Long Jun awoke the next day, he saw the fresh bread that his mother had baked. He went to the fields by the sea with his mother's cows, taking the new bread, the soft, fresh bread, with him.

He saw the beautiful woman again, and she was even more beautiful than she had been the day before. Long Jun held out his arms to her. He said, "Here is some fresh, soft bread for you. I love you more and more. Please marry me. If you do not love me too, I think I shall die."

The beautiful woman approached him. She looked at the bread in his hands and said, "You must bake your bread more. This bread is not well cooked."

The young man was very unhappy and went home.

"You are alone," said his mother. "Didn't the fairy like your bread?"

"My bread is never right for her," said Long Jun sadly. "Today she said we must bake it more. Mother, what should I do?"

His mother was a kind woman and a very good mother. She said, "Go to bed, my son. When you get up tomorrow, all will be right. I will work hard tonight to make bread that a fairy would be very pleased to eat."

At last her son went to sleep. In the morning, there was a wonderful smell in the little house from a beautiful loaf of bread. It was on the table, ready for Long Jun to take with him. He could see at once it was bread that must please any fairy!

Long Jun again went with his mother's cows to the fields with the good grass by the side of the sea. His mother stood at the door of their little house and looked after him as he walked away. She said, "This time, his beautiful woman must like the bread he is taking to her. I know that she will like it."

The poor fellow waited for many hours. He waited so long that he began to be afraid that the fairy would not come to him anymore. He waited all morning, but still she did not come.

Suddenly he remembered his cows. "Oh, dear!" he said. "It's terrible of me not to look after my mother's cows. She worked so hard to make this beautiful bread for me to give the sea fairy." But the cows were still in the field, eating grass. They had not gone away or fallen into the sea.

Long Jun waited all day. The sun began to go down; soon night would fall. He called the cows to him. On his way home, he looked back once more at the great stone in the sea. At last the beautiful woman was sitting there. She was more beautiful than ever.

Long Jun held out his mother's beautiful bread to her. He knew that it was very good. He thought that even the fairy would want it! He said, "Please, please, will you marry me? My mother has made this bread for you. No one could make any bread as fine as this. Please take it. I love you very much."

For a long time, the woman did not speak. Finally she said, "Yes, I will be your wife. Thank you for this bread. I've never seen such beautiful bread. But now you must listen to me. After we are married, you must never touch me with anything made of iron. If you ever do, I won't be able to stay with you anymore. I'll have to go back, away from you and from our house, back into the sea where I came from."

Long Jun said, "I promise I will never touch you with iron. That won't be hard for me to remember."

They were married the next day, and for a very long time they were happy.

神话

as told by
Sha Qiong

Lady Silkworm

come from the city of Ningbo in Zhejiang Province. Hangzhou, the capital of Zhejiang, is famous for its West Lake. Every spring and summer, thousands of tourists come there from all over the world. Ningbo is a small but beautiful city near the sea. During vacations I often went to the seashore, where it is quiet and the air is fresh. The people of Ningbo are good at business and warm at heart.

The folktale that I will tell you happened in Hangzhou. When I was a little girl, my grandfather told me many interesting stories. This folktale is one of them.

*L*ong, long ago, there lived in Hangzhou a girl named Agiao. When she was a little girl, her life was very happy. Her parents loved her very much, but her mother died when she was nine years old. Her father remarried and the stepmother was cruel to Agiao and her brother. She forced Agiao to do all of the housework, but Agiao was so young that she could not do it well. The stepmother whipped her until she was black and blue. Sometimes Agiao was so sore that she could not walk. Though the neighbors asked the stepmother not to be so cruel, she kept on treating Agiao badly. Instead of listening to the neighbors, she shouted and beat Agiao even more often.

One winter morning, it was very cold. The whole city was covered by a heavy snow, and it was still snowing. The stepmother told Agiao to go out and cut some grass for the sheep. Because Agiao feared her stepmother so much that she did not dare to refuse, the poor girl left with a basket on her back. She searched all day by the riverside at the foot of the mountain, but where could she find any green grass in the winter? She was tired, wet, and hungry, but she was afraid to go home and face her stepmother. She knew that if she went home without any green grass, she would be beaten and driven back outside.

She had little warm clothing on, so her whole body was trembling in the strong, cold wind. She knew that she must walk or else she would freeze. As she walked along, she noticed an old pine tree at the entrance to a valley. She pushed away its branches. To her surprise, she saw a brook with red flowers and green grass on both sides. There was no snow, no cold wind. Seeing this, she was so happy that she thought nothing of it but bent down immediately to cut some grass. She went on cutting grass until she came to the end of the brook, where she stood up to wipe the sweat off her face. Suddenly she saw a woman dressed all in white standing in front of her. The lady was smiling. She said, "Little girl, how nice to see you! Won't you come and stay with us for a while?"

Agiao looked around. To her surprise, she found herself in a different world. There were rows of white houses with trees in front of them. The leaves on the trees were green and large. There were many other women in white, singing and picking the leaves from the trees.

Agiao liked what she saw and decided to stay. She did not want to go home because she was afraid of her stepmother. She worked together with the women in white. They picked leaves from the trees and fed them to some little white worms. Slowly the little worms would grow up and spit out silk to form snow-white cocoons. The woman in white taught Agiao how to reel the shining silk from those cocoons and how to dye the silk different colors. She told Agiao that these white worms were silkworms, and the leaves that they ate were mulberry leaves. All of this beautiful silk, she said, would be used to weave colorful clouds in heaven.

Time passed quickly, and three months went by before Agiao realized it. She lived happily with the women in white and learned a lot from them. One day Agiao thought of her brother and wanted to ask him to come live there, too. Early the next morning, without telling the woman in white, she hurried back home. When she left, Agiao took some silkworm eggs and a bag of mulberry seeds with her. As she walked, she dropped the seeds along the road so that she would know the way back.

When Agiao reached home, she discovered that her father had grown old and her brother had become a young man. The cruel stepmother had died. It had been fifteen years since Agiao had left!

"Agiao! Why didn't you come home all these years? Where have you been?" her father asked.

Agiao told her father all that had happened. Her father thought that she must have met a fairy.

The next day, Agiao decided to return to the valley with her brother. When she opened the door of the house, she found that things had changed. The road was lined with mulberry trees that had grown from all of the seeds she had dropped. Agiao and her brother walked along the rows of mulberry trees until they came to the valley. Though the old pine still stood like an umbrella covering the entrance, she could no longer find a way to enter.

When Agaio and her brother returned home, they found that the silkworm eggs had hatched, so she fed mulberry leaves to the silkworms, then started to raise more of them. Later she used their silk to make beautiful cloth.

It is said that this is how the Chinese first learned to raise silkworms and use the fine thread that these tiny creatures produce. Agiao's mysterious woman in white was Lady Silkworm, the fairy in charge of the harvesting of silk.

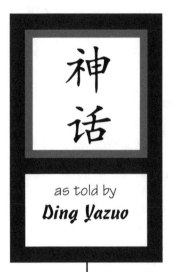

神话

The Bird with Two Heads

as told by
Ding Yazuo

I am from Zhuzhou City in Hunan Province. Hunan is famous for its hills and streams, and also is the birthplace of Mao Zedong and Liu Shaoqi. In my hometown, there are many, many stories from both ancient and recent times, and people like to listen to old folks telling these tales. One day while I was wandering in a park, I saw an elderly man telling a story, surrounded by a group of people. I joined the crowd and listened. I still recall this story, and I will tell it to you.

*L*ong, long ago, there were two men who were good friends. They treated each other very well and always did things and ate together. Later on, one of them became sick and died. The other man was very sad, and he, too, died shortly after his friend had passed away.

Several days later, the two men turned into a bird with two heads, one head for each of the friends. The bird had four legs, a couple of wings, and the two halves were joined at the mid-section. One day the bird was spotted by a hunter looking for game in the woods. The hunter aimed his gun and fired, but missed. A moment later, one of the bird's heads found some ripe fruit. Not wanting to eat the fruit first, the first head passed it to the other head. The other head, however, did the same thing, and in this way the heads kept passing the fruit back and forth. The hunter, watching this, was so moved that he slowly lowered his gun and went home.

When he arrived home, the hunter told the villagers what he had seen, and the news about this strange bird spread quickly. Eventually the emperor found out about the creature. He became so interested that he sent one of his officers to go catch it. The officer looked for the bird for many days and finally found it nesting in a tree. When he aimed his gun, however, it flew away. The officer tried many times to shoot the bird, but each time it flew away before he could fire a shot. It seemed that the bird was very fortunate.

The officer went back and thought hard. At last he had an idea. He spent the entire night weaving a net, then put it over the tree in which the bird often rested. The next day, when the bird tried to fly into the tree to have a rest, it became trapped and could not escape.

The officer sent the bird to the emperor, who was so pleased that he continually fed it delicious food. Though the bird was now in a cage, the two heads treated each other in a very friendly manner as usual. They ate, drank, and did everything together. In time the emperor became envious of their friendship, so he decided to try to separate the two heads. He gathered his ministers together and said, "If any one of you can separate these two bird heads without killing either one, I'll give you half my kingdom."

One minister answered the emperor, saying, "I will try my best to do what you wish, but I want to take the bird back home with me and keep it for at least a month."

The emperor agreed, so the minister took the bird home, feeding it delicious fruits and other food. He observed the bird every day and found that at a certain time of day, the two heads would turn away from each other. The minister realized that this was a good opportunity to carry out his plan.

The next day, when the two heads were looking in opposite directions, the minister came up close to one and quietly said, "Xu . . . ." Then he immediately went back into the house.

The other head turned around and asked, "What did the minister say to you just now?"

The head that the minister had spoken to answered, "I have no idea what he said."

In the days following, the minister did the same thing again and again. The other head always asked, "What did the minister say? Why won't you tell me?"

Day after day this happened, and the heads began to quarrel. One day they argued so violently that they turned in the opposite direction with such force that they separated. Each bird now had one head. The minister had succeeded.

The minister was very pleased. He sent the two birds to the emperor at once and asked him for half of his empire as he had promised. The emperor said to him, "Don't worry, I'll give it to you later."

Time passed, and the emperor always answered the minister in the same way. In the end the minister knew that he would not get his prize.

神话

A Lucky Girl

as told by
Xu Lijuan

I come from Hefei, Anhui. Anhui Province is in the southeastern part of China. Among the Chinese provinces, Anhui is not one of the biggest, but it is beautiful and well known for Yellow Mountain. It also produces all kinds of teas, and the Long River flows through its countryside. Hefei is the capital of Anhui. It is a small, clean, quiet city, and the population is not more than 1,000,000 inhabitants. There are few factories, so pollution is not serious, and there are many trees, so Hefei is sometimes called Green City.

When I was very young, I was told many stories about Hefei. My grandmother told me the following story when I was seven years old.

*L*ong, long ago, there was a small village on a mountain, surrounded by forests. The villagers worked very hard, but the woods were filled with wolves and other wild beasts that often harmed the villagers' sheep. There happened to be a boy named A'shan, who often drove his sheep up a small hill to a green, grassy area to feed.

One day, after A'shan had taken his sheep up to graze, he became bored. He had nothing to do all day; he just sat on the grass staring at his sheep or up at the white clouds. Sometimes he looked down at the village below. By and by his spirits became lower and lower, until he thought of an idea. He stood up and cried out, "Help! Help! There's a wolf. Help! Help! Wolf! It's eating my sheep. It'll eat me next." The villagers were working hard below, but they heard the boy's cries. They ran hurriedly up the hill with harrows and rakes. When they reached the top of the hill, there was no wolf, only the young boy laughing.

They realized that the boy had played a joke on them, and turned away angrily, saying, "Boy, you shouldn't play games like that. We are busy. If you lie like that again, no one will believe you."

A'shan said nothing, just laughed. He was amused to see so many people run up the hill in such a hurry.

The next day, A'shan brought his sheep up to the hill. Once more he became bored and in low spirits. He forgot the people's warning and once again called out, "Help! Help! Help! Here comes a wolf!"

Again the villagers ran wildly up the hill, and once more found that they had been fooled. They angrily warned A'shan that from then on they would never believe him. Again he was amused and laughed merrily.

On the third day, A'shan again brought his flock up to the hill. A fearsome wolf attacked his sheep and began to kill and eat them. How terrified the boy was! He called and called for help, but no one down in the village believed his cries. He now understood his folly, but it was too late. How sorry he was. The wolf soon turned on A'shan and killed him.

Human Nature

性格

as told by
Li Hongling

An Honest Man

I was born in the town of Fushun, which is the third-largest city in Liaoning Province. The city and its surrounding area are rich in coal. Though pollution is a serious problem, my hometown is still a beautiful city. There are many small hills around Fushun, and every spring the hills turn green and are decorated by wildflowers. Fushun is known for the Big Kitchen Reservoir, whose name comes from the fact that the Tartar tribes that later founded the Qing Dynasty once camped and cooked there.

When I was a child, my mother once told me a story that goes like this.

*L*ong ago, there was a valley where ten poor families lived. In the valley was a pool of water. One day many guests came to visit one of the families. It was rare for visitors to come to the valley, so the head of the family welcomed them and decided to have a feast. Because he was a poor man, he did not have enough plates for all of his guests, so he borrowed some from a neighbor.

After the meal, he went to the pool to clean the plates. Suddenly one of the plates slid into the water, and, though he searched and searched, he could not find it. He was very much disturbed by this and sat by the pool feeling very unhappy, trying to figure out what to do.

"Can I help you?" came a soft voice from the water.

The man looked into the water and saw a goldfish. Surprised by what he saw, he said, "Oh, a plate I borrowed from my neighbor slid into the water. How can I return it to him?"

The fish disappeared for a while, then appeared with a golden plate. He asked the man, "Is this plate yours?"

The poor man answered honestly that it was not the plate he had lost, so the fish disappeared again. After a few minutes, the fish came back with another plate, this time a silver one. Again, the poor man told the fish that it was not his plate. The fish disappeared again.

In a short while, the fish returned with the right plate. This time the man said, "Oh, yes. That's the one I'm looking for. Thank you very much!"

And what do you know! Because the man had been so honest, the fish gave him all three plates to take home to his family.

性格

as told by
Zheng Fang

Student Huang

I come from Xiantao City, Hubei. The province of Hubei has a long history, and several prosperous cultures have existed there since ancient times. Most of Hubei's major cities lie near rivers, and its major city, Wuhan, is on the Yangtze River.

My grandfather was a talkative man. In the summer it was very hot, so we often went outside to cool off and he would tell us stories. He was a kind man, so he always instructed us to treat other people well. Whenever he told us the following tale, he reminded us to do good deeds for other people.

*D*uring the Ming Dynasty, there was a poor student named Huang. When he was a boy his parents died, so he had to live alone. He studied very hard under the guidance of an old teacher so that he would learn many things and be known for his wisdom one day. Being poor, he had no light at night, so when the moon shone he went outside to read. Every morning he got up very early. Because of his dedication, he made rapid progress in his studies.

Huang was also very kind. He always helped other people when they were in trouble, bringing them a little money or giving them a hand. Because of his hard work and kindness, the people all around him knew him and liked him. They also helped him whenever they could.

The time eventually came for the emperor's exams, which were given every four years. In those days, rich young men rode horses to the exams, as they took place quite a distance away. Because Huang had no horse, he had to go to the exams on foot, starting two months before they were to be given. He took simple things with him, such as several books and a little money. On his journey he lived a hard life. During the day he walked without stopping, eating only the food that villagers gave him. At night he would sleep by the road, for he had no money to eat in a restaurant or stay at an inn.

One month later, he was still walking. To get to the exams earlier, he even walked at night. Suddenly one night, as he moved through the darkness, he saw a house with a lighted window in front of him. He was happy and surprised, because there were no other houses around. He looked up and saw many stars in the sky, then he walked up to the door and knocked. A man who looked sad opened the door to the house, which contained only a bed and a bottle. Huang bowed to the man, and the man asked Huang to be seated.

The man said, "You must be a student. Are you going to the exams?"

Huang answered, then asked, "Do you mind my troubling you with a question? Why do you appear so sad?"

The man took a deep breath and dropped his head. Then he raised his head and said with tears in his eyes, "I live alone in this house, but my wife and children live three miles away. In our village is a rich family who have five hundred horses and five hundred cows, one hundred workers, and many fields. They often cause trouble for the poor farmers just because they are rich and are friends with the officials, who care little about their cruel behavior.

"A month ago, the rich man was suddenly interested in my own small field, because it sits between two of his. He wanted to buy my field, even though I told him my family would have nothing to live on if I sold it. But one day when I went to my field I found his men working on it. When I asked him to tell them to leave, they left, but later the rich man came back with more men and ordered me to move off my land immediately. My wife and children knelt on the ground and begged him to let us be, but he just smoked and refused to hear us. When his men tried to remove us we refused, so they struck me. Two days later I was obliged to move here away from my wife and children."

Huang was so angry to hear all this that he took out his pen and paper and recorded the story to tell to a fair government official. The man very much appreciated Huang's concern and said, "I will do what I can for you." Then they went to bed for the night.

When Huang awoke in the morning, to his utter amazement he found himself lying beside a newly built tomb. He still held in his hand the piece of paper with all that had been said the previous night. Huang thought about what had happened the night before and set out in the direction of the man's wife and children, whom he found sobbing and dressed in mourning. Huang confirmed the story with the woman, then went off in search of an honest official who would be willing to hear his story. Eventually Huang found such an official, who punished the rich man and forced him to return the field to the poor farmer's wife and children so that they could live in peace.

Huang once again set out for the city to take the emperor's exams. When he finally reached the city, Huang discovered that the test was to be the next day. After a short rest he prepared himself for the exam. Early the following morning, he went to the examination hall, where he and many other young men were asked to write a detailed article on a certain subject.

Huang had studied hard so he did well, but he made one small, careless mistake on one of the characters. When the official reviewed Huang's exam, he thought he noticed an error. As he looked more closely, however, a small fly landed on exactly that spot and made the character look correct. The officer brushed away the fly, but the fly immediately landed in the same spot. The officer rubbed his eyes and finally decided that the character was correct after all. In this mysterious way, Huang's paper was judged to be perfect, and he won first place in the exam.

性格

as told by
Li Lianshan

The Legend of Wang Xiao

My hometown is near Nanyang, Henan. There are no mountains within eighty kilometers of my small town and the land is fertile, so Nanyang is a good area for farming. Some notable people were born or lived there, such as Zhang Heng, a great astronomer, mathematician, and inventor, and Zhang Zhongjing, who was an excellent doctor, writing many works on medicine. Zhang Zhongjing's tomb is located in Nanyang, while Zhang Heng's is in a town called Shiqiao. There is also a medical university named after Zhang Zhongjing in Nanyang.

This is a story about a young man and some unusual friends he made. I heard it from my grandmother.

223

A long time ago, there lived a very kind, warm-hearted young man called Wang Xiao. He was an orphan and still lived all alone when he was in his twenties.

One day he went out to see one of his friends, whose house was very far away. To get there, he had to climb a high mountain and cross several rivers, so he packed some food and set out.

While he was crossing one of the rivers he noticed a lot of ants in the water. He realized that if no one helped them, they would drown.

"Oh, poor little creatures," he thought. "They're just like human beings. I shouldn't stand by and let them be killed."

He waded over to the ants and carefully scooped them out of the water. When the ants were all safely on land, they were very thankful. One of them said to him, "Thank you for saving us. We will help you when you need us."

Wang Xiao said good-bye to the ants and went on his way to his friend's house.

When he arrived at the foot of the mountain he was hungry, thirsty, and tired, so he decided to have a rest. He sat under a tree and ate some of the food he had brought. As he was eating, he heard a strange sound coming from above his head. Looking up, he noticed several bees stuck in some sap that had flowed out of an old pine tree. As he had helped the ants when they were in danger, he also saved the lives of the bees. They were also very thankful and promised to help him whenever he was in trouble. Wang Xiao ate some more food after the bees flew away, then went on his way up the mountainside.

While he was climbing the mountain, he suddenly heard a terrible sound—the roar of a tiger. As he hurried to hide behind a big stone nearby, the tiger ran down the mountain. Wang Xiao escaped as fast as he could, fortunately finding a cave with an entrance just big enough to fit a human. He ran into the cave and found several connecting tunnels. Choosing one of these passageways, he walked along it, until he finally realized that he was lost and could not find his way out.

He had no choice except to keep walking, hoping that he would find his way out. He walked and walked and walked. To his surprise, he suddenly met an old woman who told him that she was the empress of the cave. No one, she told him, was permitted to leave the cave before separating the corn out of a large pile of corn and grass seeds. Then the woman gave him the mixture and disappeared. He began to work on it carefully, but the work was so difficult and dreary that he soon fell asleep.

When Wang Xiao awoke, he was amazed to find the mixture divided into two neat piles before him, one pile of corn without a single grass seed in it, and another pile of grass seed without a single kernel of corn. He was puzzled, wondering who had done the work while he was sleeping, but soon he found the answer. Some ants were still busy dividing the two piles. Soon they finished their work. Wang Xiao was very happy and thankful for their help and shouted to the old woman that he had finished the work. The empress was satisfied and told him that he could leave if he could find his way out.

Wang Xiao still had no idea how to find his way out, but all he could do was try. While he walked aimlessly, he noticed some bees flying before him.

"Follow us," said the bees, "and we will lead you out."

Wang Xiao was very excited when he recognized the bees as those he had freed from the amber. Following them, he walked out of the cave.

When he emerged, he found no sign of the tiger, and the sun was rising in the east. He said good-bye to the bees and went on to climb the mountain.

性格

as told by
Liu Hongwei

Let the Tiger Return to the Mountain

I am from Fugou County in Henan Province. Henan is in the northern part of China. The Jingguang railroad cuts through the middle of the province from north to south. The Yellow, or "Mother," River lies to the north of Henan. We also have many scenic places, such as the Shaolin Temple and Jigong Mountain. Most of Henan's people are farmers, and the province is famous for producing wheat and rice.

"Let the tiger return to the mountain" is a popular Chinese saying. It comes from a story about Liu Bei, who was a hero during the Three Kingdoms Period (A.D. 220–65).

*D*uring the late years of the Eastern Han Dynasty, China fell into civil war. One day Liu Bei went to Cao Cao, who later became the ruler of the Wei Kingdom, for protection after being defeated by another warlord. One of Cao's advisors told him that Liu was an ambitious man who could become a rival and block Cao's plan to unify the country. The advisor tried repeatedly to persuade Cao to kill Liu Bei, but Cao refused to do so. He said that it was time to invite to his side men of wisdom and valor instead of persecuting able and virtuous persons.

Cao showed great hospitality and respect to Liu, while the latter tried his best to hide his ambitions and demonstrate his modesty. One day Liu told Cao that he was willing to lead an army against the invading enemy, and Cao agreed. After learning the news, the suspicious advisor immediately asked for permission to see Cao. He told Cao that he would be very wrong to let Liu go.

"This would be like freeing a dragon in the sea or allowing a tiger to return to the mountain," said the advisor, "so you'd better order Liu to bring the troops back right now."

It was already too late. Liu refused to obey the orders from Cao. He left the territory controlled by Cao's troops and eventually set up his own kingdom. Later Liu did become one of Cao's chief rivals.

性格

Point to a Stone to Make It Gold

as told by
Zhang Zhiwei

The city of Anshan, in Liaoning Province, is my hometown. Anshan's iron and steel smelting factory, called Angang, is the largest of its kind in China.

The following story came from my mother.

*L*ong, long ago, there was a rich man who never felt satisfied and was eager to have more gold. One day he heard someone say that there was a magician who could point to a stone and turn it into gold.

"Would you tell me where he lives?" the rich man asked. The other man replied that the magician lived on Lao Mountain, a place known for its magical beings.

The next day the rich man left home to go to the mountain, though the way was very hard. He crossed ninety-nine bridges and climbed ninety-nine mountains before finally reaching Lao Mountain. When he arrived, he asked the magician to teach him the magic of pointing to a stone to make it gold. The magician looked at him for a few moments.

Then he said, "The magic required to turn a stone into gold is very difficult indeed. Much hard study is required. Do you still want to learn?"

"Yes, I do," said the man.

So the magician began teaching him the magic of turning stones into gold.

After a month, when they had finished, the magician said, "Now try it."

The man pointed to a tree, which immediately became gold. The magician was satisfied with his student's skills. Before the man left, the magician warned him, "You will avoid woe if you don't become avaricious."

When the man went home and saw his wife, the first thing he did was to point at his house, which turned into gold. She was very pleased and he liked this, so he forgot the magician's advice. He began pointing and soon everything in sight was gold.

Feeling thirsty he reached for a cup of tea, but when his fingers touched the cup, the cup and tea turned to solid gold. When he wanted food, it became gold also. Finally he went to bed, but his pillow and quilt were hard and cold, having turned to gold. Desperate, he called to his wife, who changed to gold before his eyes when he touched her. Surrounded by gold, the rich man died.

性格

Castles in the Air

as told by
Xu Zhihong

I am from the town of Huaibei in Anhui Province. When I was a child my grandmother often told me fascinating Chinese tales. Even now I often think of these beautiful stories. I would like to tell you one of them.

From this story I learned that I should not only think of myself, but also work to help others.

*O*nce upon a time there was a man of wealth who was ignorant and foolish. One time when he went on a visit to another rich family, he saw that they had a three-story house, grand and lofty, with spacious, bright rooms. In secret admiration, he said to himself, "I am as rich as they are. Why didn't I think of building a house like this?"

Returning to his own house, he sent for the town carpenter and asked, "Did you build the magnificent house for that family?"

"Yes, I built it," the carpenter answered.

"I want you to build me one exactly like theirs," said the rich man.

The carpenter soon surveyed the land and began construction of the house. Seeing what he was doing, the foolish man became doubtful, not knowing why the carpenter was laying bricks.

He asked, "What kind of house are you building?"

"A three-story house, of course," was the reply.

"No, no, I don't want the first two stories. You should only build the top one."

"That's impossible. How can I build the top story without the first and second stories?"

"I tell you, I'm not going to use the first two stories. You must build only the top one," said the foolish man.

The carpenter burst into laughter and stopped working, for he realized that he had been hired by a fool.

*T*he first united kingdom in Chinese history was the Qin Dynasty, and the emperor who ruled it was Qin Shihuangdi. Though he succeeded in getting power and prestige for his country, his subjects did not respect him at all because of his cruelty.

For many years Qin Shihuangdi kept looking for some potion that would prevent him from aging. We know that such a thing does not exist, but he did not believe this. He ordered his herbalists to make or find the elixir in a short time. If they failed to do so, they would lose their lives. As a result, the herbalists died one by one.

One day an herbalist named Xu came to the palace and handed in a concoction he had created under orders from the emperor. He said, "My Majesty, I have spent several months making this mixture. It is an honor to give it to you."

"Oh," Qin Shihuangdi said as he smiled. He looked at Xu for a while, then said to one of his guards, "Fetch two men for me." In a few minutes, two dying men were brought to the hall. They were fed the liquid and laid upon a table. Unfortunately for Xu, the men both soon died.

"Is this your invention?" Qin asked with a sneer.

Xu realized what would happen next. He quickly kneeled down and said, "Respected emperor, I beg you to give me a second chance. I have another way to achieve success for you. It will certainly work!"

"Why didn't you tell me this before?" the emperor asked.

Xu raised his head gradually and answered, "The only reason I did not tell you is that to do so I must have much money and many lives. We must go to an island named Peng Lai, which is thousands of miles from here. What's more, I must take 3,000 boys and girls, because the spirits there need children's bodies to make the magic potion you need."

"This is the first time I have heard such a thing," replied the emperor. "But do you dare to cheat me twice?"

"No, no." This time Xu bowed so low that his face nearly touched the ground. "How dare I cheat our emperor! I promise, if I fail to accomplish what I say, I will kill myself in front of you."

Qin Shihuangdi agreed, adding, "If you bring the life-preserving potion, I will grant you what you wish. But if you deceive me again, you won't escape my wrath."

Less than three months later, Qin Shihuangdi's soldiers forcibly removed 3,000 young boys and girls from their families and gave them to Xu. On the day they set off, Qin held a great procession at a beautiful place by the sea. That beautiful place was my hometown, Qinhuangdao. What was the result of all of this? Naturally the magic potion was not found. Moreover, Xu and the children never came back. It is said that after three months of sailing on Bo Hai Sea, they landed on an island and settled there for good.

The Young Man and the Ice

as told by
Zhang Kai

I am from Liaoyang, Liaoning. Not many people have heard of Liaoyang because it is a small city, but it is very beautiful and clean. There are many rivers and mountains, and there are trees on both sides of the streets. Because it is in the north of China, the changes of season are very definite.

In Liaoyang there are many folktales. When I was six years old, I heard this story from my grandmother. It teaches that we should be kind to our parents and friends.

*M*any, many years ago, there lived a young man in Liaoyang. The young man's father died when he was a child, so he and his mother depended on each other. The young man was very kind to his mother.

Once the mother was ill and the young man was anxious about her health. The doctor said that fish would cure the young man's mother, but at that time it was winter and the rivers were all frozen. So the young man thought and thought.

At last he came up with an idea. He went to the river and lay on the ice until it melted from the heat of his body. Then he was able to catch a fish and cure his mother.

性格

An Honest and Upright Official

as told by
Yuan Jiaqiang

I am from the city of Hefei, the capital city of Anhui Province. Anhui is in the eastern part of China and has about 50,000,000 inhabitants. It is an agricultural province, and its main crops are rice, cotton, wheat, and tea. There are many beautiful places in Anhui, such as the Changjian and Huai rivers, Chao Lake, and the Huang, Tianzhu, and Jouhua mountains. Huangshan, or Yellow Mountain, is known as one of the most beautiful places in China.

There are many folktales from Anhui. I will tell you one of these tales, which I heard from my grandmother. The events in this story happened about a thousand years ago.

*O*nce there was an honest and upright official named Bao Zheng, who was born in Hefei during the Northern Song Dynasty. When he was very young his parents died, so he had to depend on his brother for support. His brother had a son named Bao Miang but treated Bao Zheng like his own boy. Knowing that he was fortunate, Bao Zheng studied very hard and was kind to the poor.

One day, as he was reading under a tree, he saw a bull eating vegetables in a field that belonged to a poor family. Bao Zheng ran to drive the bull away. Someone told him that it was his brother's bull, but even so, he drove it away, saying, "No matter whose bull it is, it can't eat a poor man's vegetables."

Several years later, having become a young man, Bao Zheng wished to attend the great exam to be held by the emperor the following month. Hoping that Bao Zheng would pass the exam and become a government official, his brother and sister-in-law supported him. He went to the exam with Bao Miang, who had become like a brother to him.

After they arrived in Bianliang, where the exam would be held, they settled in a hotel. Another young examinee was also staying at their hotel. One day he gave Bao Zheng a topic, asking him to write out an explanation for him. Bao Zheng did so without thinking about the request. The test finally came. However, when the topic was given, he discovered that it was the very same one the young man had asked him to write about. Feeling that he had an unfair advantage over the other examinees, Bao Zheng requested another topic. At first the official did not want to give him a different topic, but at last agreed to change it. Even with this new topic, Bao Zheng did exceptionally well and was asked to be a government official.

Bao Zheng was assigned to a provincial post and immediately began investigating conditions in the area. He wandered about in shabby clothes so that no one would know he was a government official and give him false information. He was able to discover many things that had been hidden from others. Because of Bao Zheng's dedication and honesty, the emperor eventually gave him a higher position. One day Bao Zheng came to the city where his nephew, Bao Miang, was an official. Walking about in his old clothes, Bao Zheng heard people talking about some of the things Bao Miang had done. The people told him that Bao Miang was a corrupt official who had stolen a lot of money from the people.

Bao Zheng was very angry, summoning Bao Miang to answer for his deeds. After he was sure that Bao Miang had stolen from the people, Bao Zheng sent him to prison and eventually had him put to death. Yet when Bao Miang was beheaded, Bao Zheng cried, for he still loved his nephew. Though he felt very sorry for what had happened, he knew he had no other choice.

Several years later, the emperor gave Bao Zheng a still higher position in Kaifeng. It was a difficult job because the emperor's brother was in Kaifeng, and he had done many bad things. Because he was the emperor's brother, no one dared to punish him.

After Bao Zheng arrived in Kaifeng, he walked about the city. In his shabby clothes, he discovered the many dishonest and cruel things that the emperor's brother had done. He had stolen a lot of money from the people, as well as ordered his servants to find young girls for his pleasure. The people hated him, but no one dared to punish him. Bao Zheng dared to do so. After making sure that the emperor's brother had committed these crimes, he ordered his soldiers to arrest him. The emperor's brother was angry and surprised, saying, "How dare you do this? I am the emperor's brother. You must be mad!"

Ignoring his wrath, Bao Zheng sentenced him to death. After the emperor's brother was killed, Bao Zheng instructed his servants to bind him with rope while he waited for the emperor's punishment. When the imperial edict arrived, however, instead of punishing Bao Zheng the emperor praised him highly for what he had done. When Bao Zheng died, the people were very sad at having lost such an honest official. His body was sent to his hometown, Hefei, and buried there.

性格

as told by
Zhang Zhigang

Two Lives Lost for a Couple of Gold Ingots

I take pride in my home province, Shanxi. Its name comes from the fact that it lies to the east of the Taihang Mountains. As a province in the northern part of China, Shanxi is contiguous with Inner Mongolia in the north and Hebei in the south. To the west, the Yellow River flows between Shanxi and its neighbor Shaanxi.

Shanxi's people are industrious and hardworking. They love nature and life so deeply that many folktales have been handed down from ancient times to the present. The following story takes place during the Ming Dynasty. My grandmother told it to me when I was a boy.

*D*uring the Ming Dynasty there lived two beggars named Wangsan and Changszu in a village in Xiaoyi County in Shanxi Province. During their childhood they frequently begged and traveled together from one place to another. They got along so well that they would often share a piece of bread or a bowl of soup that one of them had received. Though they were poor, they never forgot to bring incense to burn in the temple and to bow down before the shrines. In time the gods noticed their piety and goodness and were deeply moved, thinking that it was only right that they should help the two beggars in some way. The God of Wealth, however, smiled and replied that though they were as brothers now, surely this would change if they became rich.

After much debate, the gods decided that they should help the two beggars, though the God of Wealth still thought that it was a bad idea. One day while Wangsan and Changszu were burning incense to the gods, to their utter amazement they found two gold ingots in the censer. The two men were overcome with happiness, realizing that these two gold bars would end their days of begging.

After the two men came to their senses, Wangsan said to Changszu, "I would like to exchange these gold ingots for some silver taels, then buy a slice of cooked beef and a calabash of wine, so we can have a good meal. Shall we?"

Changszu agreed and told Wangsan that he would wait for him to return.

Wangsan hid the ingots in his pockets and went out to the street. He had not been walking long when he began to think, "I found the gold ingots first, so I should be their sole owner. If we share them, I will only get one." The more Wangsan thought about the ingots, the more he felt they should be his alone. Finally he came to the conclusion that he must get rid of Changszu. This he could do, he reasoned, by tricking him into drinking some poisoned wine. Wangsan exchanged the gold ingots for some silver taels, then bought some cooked beef and some wine. Next he went to a drugstore and bought some poison, which he added to the wine. Then he headed back to the temple where Changszu was waiting.

Unknown to Wangsan, however, Changszu was also having second thoughts about the ingots. His reasoning was similar to Wangsan's and he concluded that he had better kill his companion and keep all the gold for himself. He hid behind the temple gate with a heavy wooden plank in his hand, waiting for Wangsan's arrival. Soon Wangsan returned carrying the beef and a calabash of wine. As he stepped across the threshold, Changszu hit him hard on the head. Wangsan fell to the ground and died.

Convinced that Wangsan was dead, Changszu threw away the plank and emptied Wangsan's pockets of the silver he had exchanged for the gold ingots. Next he sat down on the ground and proceeded to help himself to the beef and wine Wangsan had brought. After he had finished eating, Changszu stood up to go. Suddenly he felt a terrible pain in his stomach and collapsed. The poison took effect and he soon died a horrible death. Blood flowed from his nose and thick saliva from his mouth. His legs twitched for a while, then he stopped breathing. The gods above could only sigh when they saw what had happened to the two poor beggars whose good fortune ended their lives.

Mom

as told by
Lin Yang

I live in the city of Anshan in Liaoning Province. The city is near Shenyang and is famous for its steel, so it is called Steel Town. There are 1.2 million people in Anshan, many of whom work in the Angang steel factory, the largest of its kind in China. It was started by the Japanese, who carried away a lot of materials from Anshan when they occupied this part of China.

The story I will tell is unusual but true.

*I*n Anshan, in a part-time college class of young people, a woman about sixty years old with pale white hair sat in the front row. She listened carefully as the teacher spoke. People around her were surprised. "So an old woman wants to go to college," they thought.

She was never late for class. How diligent a student she was! She worked hard every evening in the classroom, impressing the teacher greatly.

On the day of the examination, the woman did not come to class. Instead, a handsome young boy sat in her seat. At first no one paid much attention to him. When the exam was handed out, the boy began to write on the test paper. When the teacher saw the boy, he was surprised, then angry, thinking that the boy was cheating. The teacher came up to the boy and addressed him. The boy paid no attention to the teacher and kept writing on the exam paper. The teacher became very angry, but just then the woman hurried in.

She told the teacher that the young boy was her son and that he was deaf. He could neither hear nor speak clearly. The teacher was amazed. The woman went on to explain that because her son could not hear, she would study the lessons herself, then teach the boy at home using a system that only the boy could understand.

In the end, the boy got a high mark on the test and his mother was very happy. The boy was very patient and intelligent, and, with the help of his mother, he earned his college diploma. When he got it, with tears in his eyes, he cried, "Mom!"

性格

as told by
**Deng
Mingyuan**

Pearl-Emerald-Jade Soup

Shenyang is a historic city and was once the capital of the Qing Dynasty. Many stories can be heard there; I happen to know a few of them. The following story was told to me by my father.

*W*hen Zhu Yuanzhang's* troops tried to overthrow the Yuan Dynasty, they were defeated in battle. Zhu fled alone, taking to the wilderness, cold and hungry, until he and his horse were worn out. Finally he fell to the ground beside a small temple and lost consciousness.

Some time later, two beggars came along. At the entrance to the temple they saw a man lying there. Finding that he was still breathing, they carried him into the temple.

They fetched twigs and straw to light a fire and laid Zhu beside it. The smoke brought him to his senses. The beggars warmed up their vegetable soup on the fire and gave it to Zhu Yuangzhang, who wolfed it down. After a while, he felt much better.

Before Zhu left, he asked the beggars, "What's the name of that soup you just gave me?"

They thought, "It's just leftovers. A name? Well . . . the cabbage and spinach are like emeralds, the rancid beancurd is like jade, and the bits of rice crust are like pearls." So they said, "It's Pearl-Emerald-Jade Soup."

"Thank you," Zhu nodded. Then he rode off.

After Zhu Yuanzhang became emperor, he grew tired of that life of luxury. In his boredom, he ordered his cooks to make him a bowl of Pearl-Emerald-Jade Soup.

When the soup was taken to the emperor, he tasted it and flew into a rage. "What's this? Pearl-Emerald-Jade Soup! Nonsense! I've had Pearl-Emerald Jade Soup before."

The cooks had to admit that they did not know how to make this soup.

Zhu thought, "Yes, my cooks are used to cooking delicacies, so I can't blame them if they don't know how to make it. But I must have that soup. Not just for myself. I'll treat my ministers and everyone in the palace to it."

Zhu's ministers looked for the beggars everywhere. Finally the two beggars were found and were taken to the palace. Zhu Yuanzhang gave them three hundred taels of silver and ordered them to cook the soup. In three days, he would have a feast for his ministers.

The beggars said to their helpers, "Buy four hundred jin of rancid beancurd, five hundred jin of spinach with roots, five hundred jin of

* Zhu Yuanzhang was the first emperor of the Ming Dynasty.

the outer leaves of cabbage, three hundred jin of coarse rice, ten jin of salt, five jin of sand, and forty buckets of dishwater."

On the third day, the palace was brightly lit. The emperor's relatives and ministers had all arrived early to wait for this treat, Pearl-Emerald-Jade Soup.

The feast started and the first bowl was offered to the emperor. He was reminded of that soup that had made him feel so good. He had been longing to taste it again. But why did it smell so bad today? No wonder people say, "To the starveling, husks taste as sweet as honey. To the replete, honey isn't sweet enough."

He said, "My dear ministers, drink this Pearl-Emerald-Jade Soup with me," then gulped it down.

Holding their breath, his ministers swallowed it mouthful after mouthful.

"Dear ministers, what do you think of this soup?" he asked.

"Delicious, delicious!" they cried.

"In that case," said the emperor, "we'll each have two more bowls."

性格

Bao Gong Tries the Stone

as told by
Zhang Ying

I was born in Shenyang, the capital of Liaoning. Though I grew up in Shenyang, I studied at the university in Harbin for four years. I now work in Tianjin, a large city near Beijing.

Liaoning Province is in the north-western part of China and is rich in natural resources. Shenyang, the capital of Liaoning, lies in the middle of the Liaohe Plain. The city is an important base of heavy industry in China, and it is also strong in science and technology.

In my childhood, we often asked my mother and father, and sometimes my grandmother, to tell us funny stories. They told us many, many stories, though now I only remember a few clearly. The following story is one of the ones they told us.

*L*ong, long ago, there was a boy whose father died, and then his mother fell seriously ill. The boy had a hard time. Every day he got up very early and took a basket of *youtao** and ran through the streets, yelling "Youtao! Youtao! Two copper coins can buy a piece of youtao!"

One day, after the boy had sold all his youtao and his basket was empty, he sat down on a stone beside the road. He counted the copper coins in the basket, "One, two, three, four. . . . " As he counted, the oil from the youtao on his hands rubbed onto the coins, making them shiny and slick. He counted exactly one hundred coins and smiled to himself. He thought that he had enough money to buy the medicinal herbs his mother needed.

The boy had worked hard all morning and was very tired, and he fell asleep against the stone. He had been sleeping there for two hours when he suddenly awoke. "Aiya! I must go to the drugstore to buy the supplies for my mother at once," he said to himself. He stood up and looked into his basket. The one hundred copper coins he had earned that day were gone! The boy was so angry that all he could do was groan and sob, crying, "Wo . . . wo . . . wo . . . . "

Just at that moment, a government official by the name of Bao Gong passed by on his horse with some of his subordinates. This Bao Gong had the reputation of being a smart, tough official who always did his duty. When he saw the boy crying sadly, he asked, "Little boy, why are you crying?"

"The money I earned from my youtao is gone," he replied.

"Who stole your money?" questioned Bao Gong.

"I don't know," answered the boy. "I fell asleep against this stone. I awoke and found all my money gone." And the boy started sobbing again, "Wo . . . wo . . . wo . . . . "

Bao Gong thought for a moment and said, "It's obvious that the stone stole your money. I'm going to try the stone and demand that it return the money to you."

People in town soon found out that Bao Gong wanted to try the stone and, thinking that this would be a very strange thing indeed, ran there to watch the fun. Soon Bao Gong was ready to begin the trial.

Bao Gong started by saying, "Stone! Admit to us that you stole this young boy's money."

---

*Youtao are deep-fried, twisted dough sticks.

Now of course a stone cannot talk, let alone reply to a question, so nothing happened.

Impatient, Bao asked the stone again, "Stone! Did you or did you not steal this boy's money?"

Once again the stone was silent.

By this time Bao Gong was getting very angry, so he screamed, "Stone! You didn't tell us the truth! Now we must punish you!"

He ordered one of his subordinates to take a metal bar and strike the stone. The man took the bar and hit the stone. "Pa . . . Pa . . . ," was the noise the stone made.

"Speak! Speak! Quickly! Tell us the truth this moment!" bellowed Bao Gong.

The many people watching laughed at the fun and said to one another, "How in heaven's name can a stone steal money? They say that Bao Gong is a clever man, but right now he looks like a fool."

Hearing the people say these things, Bao Gong became even more angry, telling them, "I am trying this stone to help the boy get his money back. Why then do you say I am a fool? Now I demand that each of you take a copper coin out of your pocket."

The people had no idea what new strange thing Bao Gong was up to, but, because he was an official and they were only peasants, they had no choice but to obey.

Next Bao Gong told his subordinates to borrow a tub and fill it with water. Then he ordered that every person, one by one, drop his coin in the water as Bao Gong watched. Bao Gong stood silently as the coins dropped, "Putong . . . Putong . . . ," taking careful note of each individual as he passed by. After one man threw his coin in, Bao Gong immediately had him arrested, saying, "Here is the man who stole the money. This man is the thief."

Everyone present thought that this was strange. How could Bao Gong possibly know that this man had stolen the boy's coins?

Bao Gong spoke and everyone listened. "This man threw a coin in the water. Oil floated off the coin, the very oil that comes from the boy's youtao. This oil is clearly visible for all to see. He is certainly the man who took the boy's money."

The man admitted that he had indeed taken the boy's coins, and Bao Gong forced him to return them all.

"Your Eminence," the people cried, "You are indeed a clever man."

性格

Two Brothers from Chu

as told by
Ye Gang

I come from the beautiful city of Wuhan in Hubei Province. It is a large city, and the longest river in China, the Yangtze, flows through it. One of the Yangtze's tributaries, the Hanshui River, also passes through Wuhan, so the city is divided into three parts by the two rivers.

What I am most proud of is the long history of the area. The culture in this place is very rich. There are many famous works written by poets and authors from Hubei.

When I was young, my parents often taught me by telling me stories. This is one of them. Of course, it's not a true story, but it taught me something valuable about the changing nature of all things, how nothing in this world, especially material things, stays constant.

*M*ore than two thousand years ago, China was not a united country but was separated into a number of small nations. One of these was called the State of Chu. During this time there were so many nations that wars constantly broke out between the countries. Many people took up arms during the Warring States Period, and soldiering became a profitable profession.

In those days, there happened to be two brothers in the Chu State who both learned a type of martial art called Jian, which is practiced with a sword. Every day they would climb a hill at sunrise and practice fighting until the sun went down. Time passed and the two brothers wanted to find out who was the more skillful.

One day the elder brother said to the younger, "How good do you think you are now?"

The younger brother replied, "I have practiced a great deal and have made a lot of progress. What about you?"

"I have also improved greatly. I think I can defeat anyone in battle now," replied the elder.

"Is that so?" said the younger. "Then I must see for myself just how good you really are."

"So you don't believe me?" the elder brother responded. "Let's fight to see who is the better."

They began to fight immediately. Because both of them were equally skilled at Jian, neither was able to beat the other. They fought and fought until the sun slowly went down. Finally the elder brother thrust and knocked the sword from his brother's hands into the valley below. The younger brother was defeated and lost his weapon.

Now that they had stopped fighting, they began to think about how to recover the sword that had fallen into the valley. They both agreed that they should try to find it that evening, because in the morning they might not remember where it had landed. It soon became very dark and they wondered what they should do. Finally, after thinking the matter over, the elder brother drew his dagger and made a mark on the rock at exactly the place where the sword had fallen off the mountain. Then they left with the intention of returning the next morning and using the mark to find the sword.

The next day, they found the mark and easily located the lost sword. The younger brother was impressed and remarked, "Brother, you have truly thought of a good way to find a lost sword."

Several months later, the younger brother had some business in another town and had to sail a ways down the Yangtze River, so he employed a small boat for the journey. The river was very wide and the boat was slow, so he decided to practice Jian to pass the time. While he was practicing, his sword suddenly slipped from his hand and fell into the river.

The boatman told the young man to dive into the water immediately and look for his sword.

The young man replied, "It's no problem. Don't make a fuss. I can take it out when we arrive at our destination." He took a small knife and made a mark on the side of the boat where the sword had fallen into the water. Then he said proudly, "I will be able to recover the sword with the help of this mark."

The others on the boat laughed at him, but he did not mind. When they arrived at their destination, the young man jumped into the water precisely where the mark on the boat indicated that his sword had fallen. To his dismay, he could not find his sword. He thought hard about the matter, but could not understand why the sword was not where he thought it should be.

性格

as told by
Zhang Zhaobin

Learn to Walk Bridge

My hometown, Handan, lies in the southern part of Hebei Province. Handan is an important city in Hebei. It is on a major rail line, and every year a lot of cotton is grown in the countryside around Handan, which is made into cotton cloth in the city's factories. There is plenty of coal in Hebei, which is transported to other parts of China. In addition, millions of tons of iron ore are transformed into steel in Handan.

Handan is an interesting place to visit, for it was once the capital of the Zhao Kingdom. Some pleasant sites worth visiting in the city are Changtai Park and Jingniang Lake. My story, told to me by my teacher when I was in middle school, is about an unusual bridge in town.

A long time ago, when Handan was the capital of the Zhao Kingdom, there lived a rich man near the city. Though he had a lot of money and owned many fields, he was unhappy because people said that he walked in a very, very strange way. This bothered him a lot, but he had no idea what to do about his odd manner of walking.

One day someone told him that the way the people in Handan walked was very pleasing to the eye. He thought to himself, "If this is true, I'll go there and learn how to walk. Then no one can say that my walk is ugly, and no one will laugh at me anymore. Yes, I must go there."

The next morning, he set off for Handan with some food and water. By the time he arrived in the city, his food and water were gone. At the gate of the city, the rich man saw a hunter striding along with his bow and arrows slung across his back. The rich man thought, "Aha! Great! How strongly and proudly this man walks. I surely can learn from him!"

The rich man entered the town, following the hunter and imitating his walk. As he walked, however, he found many people in the street laughing at his awkwardness, so he stopped.

He was very hungry and caught sight of a restaurant on the other side of the street. He entered the restaurant, ordered some food and wine, and began to eat. As he was eating his meal, he noticed how skillfully the waiter moved between the tables. He thought, "Oh, how elegantly this man walks. I can surely learn from him."

The rich man began to walk behind the waiter, but he could not walk as quickly as the waiter and kept knocking other customers and bumping into tables. At last he was driven out of the restaurant.

Back in the street, he did not know where to go, so he had to wander here and there. Suddenly he saw a young girl walking in front of him. "What a pretty girl," he thought. "How beautiful she is when she walks."

The rich man stared at the girl and followed her. The girl became worried and walked faster and faster. The man also walked faster and faster, until finally the girl began to run and cried, "Help! Help!" Some young people heard the girl and stopped the man. He wanted to explain, but before he could say a word he was taught a good lesson.

When he stood up, he thought, "I have wasted an entire day! I can't seem to learn how to walk beautifully. But . . . How did I walk before?" He had forgotten how to walk and had to crawl the whole way home.

This story has been told from one generation to another for many years. No one knows whether it is true, but there is still a bridge named Learn to Walk Bridge in Handan. When people see this bridge, they cannot help but think of the foolish rich man in the story.

Continually Promoted

as told by
Hu Fangren

come from Longhai Town, Shaoyang City, Hunan Province. My hometown is beautiful. Around the town, there are many mountains, and a small river flows softly all year long, winding its way through town from east to west. In the spring, the mountains near Longhui are a sea of flowers, so many that you cannot decide which ones to pick. In the hot summer, many people like to go swimming in the river, and the air is full of the sounds of children playing in the water. In the fall, the fields are transformed into tall, golden waves of wheat ready for the harvest.

One evening when I was eight, my grandfather told me a story by moonlight. He told me that this story took place during the Ming Dynasty, when Zhu Yuanzhang was emperor.

*I*n the days of the Ming Dynasty, it was hard for people to make a living, and the only way to a better life was to pass an examination held by the emperor himself. If one passed the exam, the future would be bright and a good position could be obtained in the government.

During this time, there was a gentleman named Zhang Haogu in my hometown, whom the local people all knew to be very vain. Though he always spoke very highly of himself, he was a very common man in other people's eyes. Zhang Haogu regarded himself as a great man and enjoyed hearing good words about himself.

One day a monk came to town. The monk knew of Zhang Haogu, but Zhang had never heard of nor seen the monk. One morning they happened to meet in the street.

"Oh, my goodness! What an uncommon man," the monk shouted upon seeing Zhang Haogu.

Very surprised but very happy, Zhang Haogu looked at the monk, whom he had never seen before, and asked, "How can you tell?"

The monk replied, "From your appearance, especially your face, eyes, and ears. I can tell that you will pass the emperor's examination if you take it." Then he added, "This year's examination will be given in a few days, so you'd better set off to take it."

Zhang Haogu was delighted. He gave the monk much money and told him, "If I pass the examination, I'll give you more."

Other people in town laughed at what had happened, for they knew Zhang Haogu did not know much at all. Unconcerned, Zhang Haogu set out for the capital city, Chang'an, for the examination. After riding a horse day and night for three days, Zhang Haogu finally reached Chang'an. It was night when he arrived and he had no idea where the examination was to be held, so he decided to look for it.

Riding by the light of the moon, he passed through the streets of the city in search of the examination hall. Suddenly he came upon a group of soldiers in a procession. Zhang Haogu stopped his horse, but in no time he was surrounded.

Astonished, he shouted, "Don't delay me! I'm going to take the emperor's examination, and I'm going to take second place."

Hearing this, the soldiers made way for an elderly man to approach Zhang Haogu. This man happened to be a Ming official, Wei Zhongxian, who was on a routine inspection of the streets of the capital.

Wei Zhongxian was surprised to see Zhang Haogu. "This man must be an unusual man, otherwise he wouldn't dare to say such things," he thought to himself. So he gave Zhang Haogu a card with "Wei Zhongxian" written on it. Zhang Haogu thanked the minister and continued searching for the examination hall.

He finally found it, but he was told that the examination had ended an hour before. When he handed them the card, they were shocked. They thought that he must be a relative of Wei Zhongxian. Fearing terrible consequences if they did not give him the examination, they allowed him to write the examination paper.

Ten days later it was announced that Zhang Haogu had taken second place in the examination. Others, including Wei Zhongxian, were shocked. Zhang Haogu was appointed to a high position in the court. He sent a letter of thanks to Wei Zhongxian, and Wei wrote back, praising him for his "abilities." The news that Zhang Haogu had taken second place was quickly sent back to Longhai, and all of the people were shocked.

Zhang Haogu worked in the emperor's palace but, because he could not read or write very well, he always dictated his work to his secretary. As time went by, the secretary began to suspect that Zhang Haogu could not read. Five years later, Wei Zhongxian held a banquet to celebrate his seventieth birthday. Many high officials were invited, including Zhang Haogu, who wanted to present a handsome gift to Wei. He instructed his secretary to write a note of congratulation on a beautiful piece of silk cloth. Instead, however, the secretary wrote some slanderous lines on the cloth, hoping to find out if Zhang Haogu could read them.

Zhang looked the lines over and praised them, as if he had read them perfectly, then sent them off to the minister. When Wei Zhongxian received the cloth, he knew that Zhang was an ignorant man. However, fearing the emperor's wrath should he denounce Zhang, he only hid the cloth in a closet. Soon after this, Wei himself was thrown into prison. It was said that he had conspired to kill the emperor.

One day, while the emperor's servants were searching Wei's house, they found the cloth that Zhang had given to the official. Amazingly, the words written on the silk seemed to prefigure the arrest of Wei and demonstrate Zhang Haogu's loyalty to the emperor. These things became known all around the country. As a result, Zhang was appointed to the top position in the nation, which happened to be advisor to the emperor himself. In this way, a silly man attained the second-highest position in the land.

性格

as told by
Wu Zhihao

The Bow on the Wall, the Snake in the Cup

I am from Hainan, the youngest and smallest province in China. It is in the southeastern part of China and was formerly a part of Guangdong. It became an independent province in 1988. In the five years since Hainan became a province, our economy has grown considerably. I live in Sanya, the second-largest city in Hainan. It is beautiful there, and every year Sanya attracts thousands of tourists.

Where there are people, there are stories, and my hometown is no exception. I first learned this story from my mother when I was a child. It is still told among the people, so almost everyone in my hometown knows this story. It is said that this story has been handed down for centuries.

*L*ong, long ago, there was a man named Le Guang who always invited his good friends to his home to have a drink. Once he invited a friend to have a drink at noon. They were having a lively, fine time, when suddenly his friend turned sullen and withdrew from the table abruptly. Le Guang was puzzled. He thought that there must be something strange about his friend, but he asked nothing.

After that meeting, his friend failed to call on him for several days, which was unusual. Le Guang wanted to know the reason, so he sent a servant to his friend's house to find out what was wrong. The answer was strange: his friend was seriously ill from having drunk a snake in the cup at Le Guang's home.

How could a snake have been in the cup? Le Guang could hardly believe it. He meditated on this mystery and was determined to bring it to light. He sat in the same place as his friend had sat. He poured himself a cup of wine and glanced in it. To his surprise, he too saw a small snake swimming in the cup! He gazed at it astonished, then raised his head. Looking at the wall, he suddenly burst into laughter. There it was! The snake his friend had drunk was hanging on the wall!

Knowing the truth, Le Guang decided to cure his friend's illness. He thought and thought, then came up with a good idea. He invited his friend to drink again, promising this time to drag the devil of a snake out of his stomach. His friend feared coming, but at last he came, looking lifeless and on the brink of death.

Le Guang smiled but said nothing at first. He seated his friend in the same place as before, poured him a cup of wine, and bade him drink. No sooner had his friend looked into the cup than his face turned white as a sheet. There was a snake in the cup again! He trembled, unable to say a word.

With a smile, Le Guang said, "Don't be so scared, my dear friend. Let's play a magic game, and you will find out what kind of a snake you have drunk." Le Guang went to the wall, took down a bow that was shaped like a snake, and said, "Now look in your wine carefully."

His friend lowered his gaze into the cup, but the wine was clear and there was no sign of the snake. "Where did the snake go?" he said to himself. Suddenly he cried, "Oh! The reflection of the bow played this joke on me!"

Soon he recovered from his illness and again came to Le Guang's house to have a drink. Of course, Le Guang was pleased. After all, they were good friends.

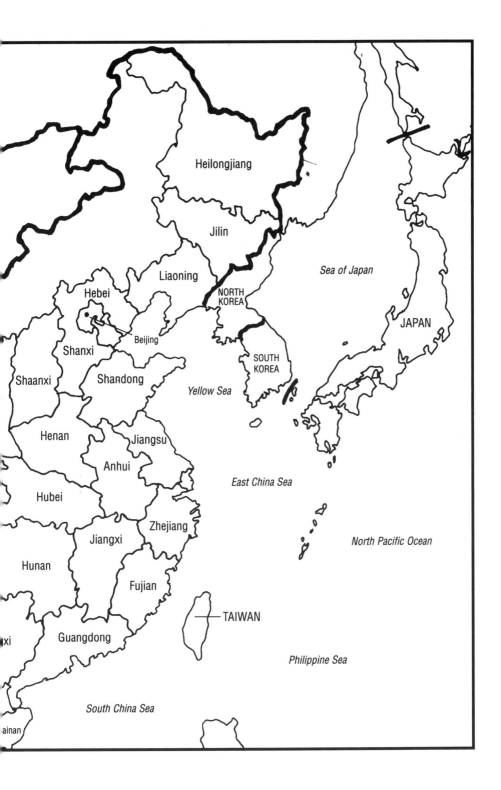

Heilongjiang

Jilin

Liaoning

Hebei

Shanxi

Beijing

Shaanxi

Shandong

Henan

Jiangsu

Anhui

Hubei

Zhejiang

Jiangxi

Hunan

Fujian

xi

Guangdong

ainan

NORTH
KOREA

SOUTH
KOREA

Yellow Sea

East China Sea

TAIWAN

Sea of Japan

JAPAN

North Pacific Ocean

Philippine Sea

South China Sea

Pinyin Pronunciation Guide

The Pinyin system is used for most Chinese words in this book. Letters with unfamiliar pronunciations appear below. Other letters approximate standard English sounds.

Vowels

a	as in f*a*ther
ai	as in *i*dol
ao	as in n*ow*
e	as in b*oo*k
ei	as in sl*ei*gh
i	as in h*ea*t
	as in d*i*vine
	(when preceded by *c, s,* or *z*)
	as in h*er*
	(when preceded by *ch, r, sh,* or *zh*)
ia	as in y*ar*n
ian or **yan**	as in *yen*
iu	as in tr*io*
ie	as in *ear*
o	as in f*o*r
ou	as in sm*o*ke
u	as in pl*u*me
	as in p*u*t
	(when the syllable ends with *n*)
	as in German '*ü*'
	(when preceded by *j, q, x,* or *y*)
ui	as in sw*ay*
uo	as in w*a*ter

Consonants

c	as in si*ts*
j	as in *joy*
q	as in *ch*eer
x	as in *sh*ore
z	as in ki*ds*
zh	as in *ju*ngle